WE'RE NOT Sixteen ANYMORE:

A Baby Boomer's Adventures with Online Dating

BECKY ANDERSEN

Georgia

Published in the United States by WriteLife Publishing
(an imprint of Boutique of Quality Books Publishing Company)
www.writelife.com

978-1-60808-156-1 (p)
978-1-60808-157-8 (e)

Library of Congress Control Number: 2016931147

Book design by Robin Krauss, www.bookformatters.com

Cover design by Kris Pittman , Breakaway Designs

I dedicate this book to whoever invented cyber-dating;
to loved ones everywhere who encourage someone
to live life to its fullest;
and especially to my beloved family and friends.

Welcome to the Sixties

I never, ever thought I would be doing something at age sixty that I had last done at age sixteen. Every other activity I used to do when younger has gradually morphed from ease and enjoyment to discomfort and embarrassment.

Case in point: When I was in my teens, I could hardly wait my turn to jump on a trampoline! I could easily scramble up and on to the bed of the trampoline. Sometimes, if there was a small audience I wanted to impress, I'd grab the metal base and somersault over the springs onto it. When I was recently at my daughter Alyssa's house, her three-year-old son begged me to climb on board his trampoline and bounce with him. Like any loving grandmother, I complied. It took a few minutes to realize my teen agility was non-existent, then another fifteen minutes to find a small stepstool that I could use to climb up, but then I was set.

"MoMo, bounce me!" my little Tristan yelled. What fun this would be for both of us, I thought! I gathered myself for a giant leap to "send" him, bent my knees, and shot upward, probably all of two inches. I discovered very quickly that while some parts of my body *did* lift up a bit, other parts of my body obeyed the laws of gravity and stayed put. Let's just say I will never again drink any liquids *if* and when I get back on a trampoline.

That should have taught me that I am *not* sixteen anymore. For really physical activities, I have become very aware of that. But the real epiphany came to me one day when I found myself speeding to the mall. I always speed—a little bit—when I go to the mall to shop. I might miss some big bargain if I dawdle. This time, though, I wasn't on my way for any big bargain. When I thought of what I was about to do, my stomach felt like it had on the trampoline, and I slowed down and almost turned around. I was shaky, nervous, and totally scared to death. I was about to do something else besides jumping on a trampoline that I hadn't done since my teen years: I was on my way to meet a *date*. Only this time the date wasn't someone I'd had a crush on in high school. This date was due to the twenty-first century's technological advances: it had come about through *online dating*. Emotionally, I was still twentieth century.

In the 1950s and 1960s, my dad worked for a company that frequently transferred him to a different part of the state. There were also times we needed a bigger house as the family grew. Sometimes that involved a move to a different school district within the city. So for most of my primary education, I never went to one school two years in a row. I was the new girl every year. The new girl named Becky

Button – and there was always someone in the class who smirked at my name.

When I was sixteen, my family moved from the second-largest city in Iowa back to my parents' small hometown. I wanted to stay put. At sixteen, I wasn't given a choice. I was devastated. It was one thing to come to visit my grandparents and other relatives, but quite another to actually live there.

But by the time school started in the fall, I'd had a change of heart and was determined to make a good first impression in order to get friends. There was one good thing being back in the family's hometown: I wouldn't have to worry about my name being made fun of. There were lots of Button relatives who went to school there. So I spent quite some time picking out my new clothes to wear that first day. Finally I was comfortable with how I looked, at least until I got to school. One thing my new town didn't have, I discovered, was a school with air conditioning. New school clothes were designed for cool autumn days, but in Iowa, those days don't usually occur until the middle or end of September. My first day of junior year at the high school, and I was a miserable and sweaty mess.

Had I ever had more than one year to cultivate a boyfriend relationship with someone, it would have had to be with someone quite mature for his age and who had great foresight. Someone who could have looked at the new girl and seen beyond the weight (perfect for a girl five feet ten, when I was only five feet four) and who was attracted to the hair color called dishwater blonde. Someone who could ignore the gap between my front teeth—a gap big enough to stick a straw through and still be able to smile—and who thought thick-lensed glasses made my dull hazel eyes shine. Now I was going to be in one place for two years. I felt hopeless. Then a miracle occurred.

Mother Nature took pity on me—or else it was the exercise and hectic pace of the activity-driven lifestyle that comes with being in everything small-town schools offer—but by my senior year, I had thinned down to an appropriate weight for my height. I also got contact lenses, and dyed my dishwater blonde hair with hair color. And a few boys developed an interest in me.

I dated five different boys in high school. My younger siblings found that their oldest sister's forays into the world of dating opened up a whole new avenue of teasing. Whenever a date picked me up or dropped me off, my little brothers and sisters would spy on me. More often than not, my embarrassed date and I, standing at the door to say good night, would hear "smooching" sounds accompanied by giggles and snickers. I'd erupt in Type A fury and go storming into the house, hollering to my parents, "Those *brats* are driving me crazy!" and leave my poor date to disappear quietly into the night. Maybe that's why I averaged only one date apiece with four of those five boys.

But the fifth boy was *the one*. He was the 1971 senior class president, a brown-eyed, dimple-cheeked young man with curly dark hair, and he made me laugh. He adored me, and I adored him in return. I married Harold Beaman just a few weeks before I turned twenty-one, and for thirty-seven years, we lived a life full of fun and laughter with our two daughters, Brooke and Alyssa. I had a job I loved at the local private college, Simpson College, in Indianola. The girls grew up to be fantastic young women, and Harold had his dream cabin in southern Iowa where he would hunt, fish, and just relax. Everything was perfect until our life together was abruptly cut short by his unexpected and sudden death when he was only fifty-seven.

All of this flashed through my mind as I was driving to meet this date. It had been over forty years since I'd dated. I had no idea what had possessed me to let myself get signed up on a dating website. Now I was about to meet a total stranger, even though we'd been paired up through the magic of cyber-psychoanalytical facts. Dating at age sixty? *Good grief,* I thought, *what's this guy going to think when he sees an old woman walk in? For that matter, what am I going to think when I meet* him? *What will he look like in person? What do I say? How do I act? Who's going to pay for the date?*

I think I want my mommy!

The road to dating at age sixty actually started on a summer's day in 2012. It was my birthday. I was coming to grips with the fact that I was indeed, now, sixty years old. When people started emailing or calling me up to wish me happy birthday, and then remarked that they couldn't believe how *old* I was, that fact slapped me hard in the face.

There was no way around it. I was sixty. Most definitely "over the hill."

This birthday bothered me more than my last major one. At age fifty, I could tell myself I *possibly* had another fifty years in me. After all, practically every day, there is some news about someone celebrating a one hundredth birthday. Granted, they're not *really* celebrating in the sense of jumping up and down, gleeful that they hit that magic mark. But it is an accomplishment. Then the reporter shows the birthday "boy" or "girl" in a wheelchair or bed, and explains to what the centenarian attributes this longevity. Usually it was habits that I don't have, so for a day or two I'd wonder if I had time to change my lifestyle so *I* could get interviewed in another fifty years.

But to think I had another *sixty* years in me? I'm pretty much an optimist, but I'm also a realist. I can hope I'll live long, but in reality, odds are I'll not live another sixty years. And what if I did? I tried to imagine a one-hundred-and-twenty-year-old Becky. It wasn't pretty. But on the other hand, at that age I would definitely be past caring about my looks, and, *finally*, I could eat anything I wanted . . . *if* I still had my teeth.

Remember pre-pubescence, when the boys were separated from the girls, and we had to watch a movie about what was going to happen to our bodies in the next few years? I think senior citizens should lobby for a movie designed for anyone about to enter menopause, to tell them what kind of bodily changes *we're* going to experience. The first time I looked as close in a mirror as a near-sighted old lady can get, in order to wipe a smudge on the bridge of my nose, I discovered that the "smudge" was a unibrow that I'd never had before. I was horrified.

Egads, I was sixty, widowed, and had an underlying fear of growing "old" and being alone. Who would tell me if I had hair growing out of my ears? Who would help me zip up a back zipper? What if karma got even with me for all the times I'd laughed at the "Help, I've fallen and I can't get up" commercial, and that really *happened* to me? Are there designer dresses with Velcro?

Feeling slightly—all right, *hugely*—depressed, I spent the morning of my sixtieth birthday looking at pictures of myself. Younger me. Me as a baby, as a bride, as a new mother. Oh, where had the time gone? For that matter, where had the young woman in those pictures gone?

I looked in a mirror, and for the first time, empathized with the wicked queen in *Snow White*. I could understand her—what's really wrong with wanting to be the fairest in the land? I mean, as long as there are very light shades of blonde hair color, every woman can be the "fairest." But would it be so wrong to wish for a firmer neckline, creamy skin, and less wrinkles?

I had no idea where all those wrinkles had come from. I could call a few of them "laugh-lines," but the rest of the crevices on my face I would have to call after the names of gorges in Grand Canyon National Park. Brown spots on my arms and legs had once been identified as cute freckles. I knew where they had come from: iodine and baby oil lathered on for hours of tanning at the local pool when

I was in my teens, way before anyone heard of "SPF." While I regret trying to tan that way, I'm glad that at least we call them "sun spots" rather than as the disgusting "liver spots" that my grandparents' generation referred to them.

I continued my inspection. Where had the muscles gone that used to keep my skin so taut? My skin was hanging on my body like crepe paper the day after a party—that was, except for the parts of my body that were curvy. Only those curves were not wrinkle-free due to muscles, and were also not supposed to be spilling over the top of my jeans. What good was it to get older?

Well, I had to admit there were *some* perks to turning older. I would finally be eligible for all of those money-saving discounts that I'd thought I would get at age fifty-five, but then found were bumped up to another age category!

With the prospect of turning a year older being a real downer, I happily accepted an invitation to a birthday dinner from my brother and sister-in-law. A quiet birthday dinner would be nice for a change, instead of heating up frozen diet entrees. The evening of my birthday, I arrived at their house and rang the doorbell.

My sister-in-law flung open the door. She was dressed in a mini-skirt and go-go boots, and her hair was flipped up on the ends. Before I had time to process what I saw, a roar of "WELCOME TO THE SIXTIES!" reverberated from the interior. I was instantly transported back to the 1960s. Ga-roovy!

I was given a choice of what to wear: either a mini-skirt, or a long chiffon dress that looked like something the Supremes had worn. It was an easy choice—I had barely had the knees and thighs to wear a mini-skirt when I was sixteen. They were now the repositories for the upper two-thirds of my body's gravity issues. I changed into the chiffon, and went out to meet the guests.

There were my family of three brothers, two sisters, parents, in-laws, nieces, nephews, one of my own daughters, and dearly loved high-school friends! Only they were dressed as long-haired hippies, characters that looked like they were straight out of *Mad Men*, flower children, and go-go dancers, and wore Afro-wigs, tie-dyed shirts, white boots, and Nehru jackets.

My follicularly challenged brothers had hair again, and it was long hair this time! The men in the group, notorious for rolling their eyes at playing dress up, were actually posing for pictures and flexing imaginary muscles. Some guys were in headbands, or leather jackets, or anything remotely 1960s-ish. The house was decorated in mid-sixties iconic peace symbols, with vintage cigarette ashtrays and lava lamps to add to the fun.

I was handed a faux roach (not the bug!), but put the wrong end in my mouth. Candy cigarettes' pretend ashes were tapped against giant turquoise or red ashtrays. "In-A-Gadda-Da-Vida" and other hits from the sixties were blasting from an old radio, and everyone was talking, laughing, and dancing. Even my birthday cake was a symbol of the sixties—a great big yellow happy face!

It was a fantastic way to feel young again, and to time-travel back to my teen years. It was the best party I'd ever had. It was certainly more fun acting like I was sixteen when I was sixty than it had been actually being sixteen. Now I could drink! I hated to have the party end.

So, when less than a year later, I had the opportunity to experience something else I hadn't done since my teen years, I jumped on the bandwagon. Well, *jumped* might not be the right term, exactly. I was pushed, maybe. Prodded, more likely. I wasn't too enthusiastic at first, because this was going to be outside my comfort zone. I had the chance to be "with it" again, just like a Baby Boomer of old. Only now it would be in the twenty-first century—and it would be called *electronic dating*.

Baby Boomer

Once upon a time, had I heard of someone over the age of forty dating, I would have been horrified. Who would *date* at that age? And *why*? Just the thought of two *old* people kissing was disgusting!

I remember the first time the thought of older people doing anything that younger people could do occurred to me. It was around my freshman or sophomore year of high school. One day, a friend of mine came to school crying. She was immediately surrounded by a whole group of us girls, hovering, wondering what was so horribly wrong. Did she flunk a test? Did she just break up with her boyfriend? Did she get a zit?

She sobbed and hiccupped, and finally was able to blurt out: "My mom and dad are going to have a . . . a . . . " A *what*? We were all holding our breath.

" . . . A bayyyy-beeee!" She almost collapsed in grief.

Seven collective jaws dropped open. A *baby*? My friend was the youngest of three. This was the same girl who had already gotten to be a bridesmaid for one of her older sisters (a fact the rest of us friends were jealous about), and she was already an aunt! And she was telling us her parents were going to have a *baby*?

Her mom and dad were *grandparents*, for heaven's sake! They couldn't have a baby. Yuck! One girl, in a most ineffective attempt at consolation, told my friend that she *had* to be wrong. There was no way people could have a baby at *that* age, she said. (They were in their early forties.)

You see, we might have been young, but we knew all about life. After all, we'd had to sit through *the* movie three years before—the one every twelve-year-old girl in the 1960s had to watch in health class—so we had an idea of how girls or young married women could get pregnant. But people over the age of forty? Nahhhh. That wasn't in the movie. Our friend had to be wrong. The idea of someone's parents *"doing it"* was almost ridiculous. Or so we thought then. Never mind that as the oldest of six, I never bothered to wonder how all those babies appeared at our house!

Oh, arrogant youth, thy name is Becky! I can say that now as I look back. But growing up Baby Boomer, it seemed as though the world revolved around us young people, and we were okay with that. We knew everything. We learned it from television!

Growing up in the 1950s meant becoming addicted to that fairly new invention, the television set. Sitting in front of the TV, my generation was subjected to something called "commercials," a lot of which had to do with food and beverages. Along with other kids my age, we began to associate TV with food. Sunday evenings were popcorn night because *Walt Disney Presents* was on. *The Wizard of*

Oz automatically meant popcorn balls. Friday nights we were allowed to eat our fish sticks in front of the TV so we could watch *Kukla, Fran and Ollie* or *The Perry Como Show*. And Saturday mornings found us seated on the floor in front of the TV, as if our little hind ends were glued there, in order to watch *Mighty Mouse, Howdy Doody,* or *Rin Tin Tin*. Anytime a commercial came on the television set that was geared more for adults, we kids changed from zombie-eyed captives of the TV to the world's fastest sprinters. Olympians couldn't match our speed as we raced from the living room to the only bathroom in the house and/or the kitchen refrigerator in order to get snacks for the next segment of the show. And the first one back got the primo spot, as close as possible to the tiny TV screen.

As we got older, we expanded our knowledge through game shows and newscasts. Our horizons broadened, without us ever leaving our own home. Oh, such a smart thing to do!

Take fashion, for another example. Twiggy and Jean Shrimpton were our fashion idols. Anything British was "in." We wore tent dresses in electric-blue paisley or hot pink and orange florals. These beautiful creations hid the chubbiness of adolescence. They also drew gasps from parents who thought they were about to be grandparents the first time they saw their daughters in the billowing fashions.

We also wore mini-skirts so short that they were probably the reason some girls my age *did* get pregnant—or the crude "knocked up" in 1960s lingo—although the slogan "Make Love, Not War" may also have had something to do with it.

Some people my age experimented with drugs. My girlfriends and I experimented with *cosmetics*: white pearly lipsticks, thick black eyeliner, and blue, blue eyeshadow. That look was so popular then that it can still be seen today—on *The Walking Dead*.

As Baby Boomers born between the years 1946 and 1964, we believed we were far superior intellectually to anyone our parents' age or older. The sci-fi thriller *Logan's Run* was our version of the current *Hunger Games*. Youth was strong, smart, and able to rule.

But then something happened to me. To a lot of Baby Boomers, as a matter of fact. Just aging would have been bad enough, but did life have to change so drastically? Why did so many of those drastic changes have to be about technology? My current house, built a year before the millennium, is better built for the future than I am. It has more wires in it than Spaghetti Works has noodles for a week-long all-you-can-eat buffet. Whether we Boomers like it or not, the key to the future is in cyberspace.

Somewhere between *Sesame Street*'s Big Bird V-Tech computer for ages three and up in the 1980s, and the Apple Watch of today, our children's generation suddenly became more technologically savvy than most of us Boomers would admit. It wasn't just technical stuff, either. I worked at a college and overheard matter-of-fact conversations about sex that were way more provocative than any racy romance novel I'd read. They were worldly and more informed about countries, religions, the environment, and politics than us Boomers ever were, mainly because of the advent of the Internet and the World Wide Web.

While time moved on, evidently Baby Boomers didn't. Remember when about the only acronym you heard was "IBM," short for International Business Machines? Now there are dictionaries with nothing *but* acronyms listed, and most of them are now for texting. The first time I hurriedly emailed one of my children some sad news about an acquaintance, I ended the missive with "LOL"—for "Lots of Love." My daughter called me to say she failed to see anything funny about an illness, and then had to explain to her befuddled mother that "LOL" now means "Laugh Out Loud." Can't people talk or write in complete words anymore? Who made all this shorthand up? Now before I even figure out what an acronym stands for, it becomes obsolete, and is replaced with something new.

It's certainly true that what goes around, comes around. It's payback time for all those moments I felt smarter than my parents. I can now empathize with the hundreds of generations before me who have plaintively whined, "If it ain't broke, don't fix it!" As a once-progressive Baby Boomer, I tried to keep up with the times. But times definitely do change, and change is good, right? Well, maybe.

With Friends Like These...

The winter following my sixtieth birthday party, my eighty-year-old mother started gently hinting about me finding "friends."

I had flown down to Florida to visit my parents, where they flock with other snowbirds in a beautiful condo to get away from the Iowa winters. It was an ego boost for me to be the youngest person there. It was relaxing walking the beach, picking up shells, and looking for dolphins. It also had its thrills. You've never experienced the kind of electrifying buzz I got riding in the back seat of the car while my dad raced around what he called (expletive deleted) "jerks" while driving to four p.m. supper at a favorite restaurant in order to get the "good seats." I also enjoyed just being able to sit and talk to my mom and dad or watch TV, if Dad ever changed channels away from the stock market.

One day, while TV was on, Mom suddenly got excited, shouted, "Look!" and pointed at the television screen. All I saw were some old people on a commercial. For a minute, I thought she must have recognized a friend. But it was just an ad for a dating site especially designed for more "mature" (*old*) people.

I looked at her. "Are you thinking of dumping Dad?" I joked.

"No, no, it's just . . . interesting." She said *interesting* with the "ing" part trilling upward into a quasi-question, designed to rouse my curiosity. (My mom is very good at leaving sentences open at the end for any of her kids to fill in the blank.)

Okay. I remembered that I was one of the youngest people—and now, years after my husband's death, the only single person—in this condo right now. If this trip down here was going to consist of probing various commercials, I could play along . . . as long as we didn't get into too much heavy stuff. "Well, I don't know about interesting, but can you believe how *disgusting* that commercial is about the bear who needs soft toilet paper to wipe?" I said.

"Well, I'm talking about getting *friends*," Mom countered.

My always-reticent dad piped up: "She means *man* friends!"

"Oh." I was shocked. I hadn't seen that coming. I'd never even thought about friends specifically as men or women. Man friends? Did that mean something like boyfriends? All I could blurt out was: "No, thanks, I'm good."

Out of the corner of my eye, I saw Mom glare at Dad and give him THE LOOK. That LOOK could bore through the soul of its victim, and even peripherally spread to include anyone nearby. When she had turned THE LOOK on me, or on one of my five siblings while we were growing up, it had been common for not only the culprit to freeze and apologize, but for a chorus of apologies to reverberate through the house, issued in fear from any nearby innocent bystanders.

Guilty or not, the power of THE LOOK still worked. Dad and I both apologized at the same time. I made it through the rest of the visit without having any more dating commercials pointed out.

Once I was home, however, the gentle suggestions continued from other members of the family. I'd underestimated the determination they had to make me "happy" again. Evidently Mom and my daughters had watched *Fiddler on the Roof* one too many times, because they decided to become cyber Yentes and get a "friend" for me—on the Internet.

Right before my sixty-first birthday, my daughter Brooke confessed to me that she'd set up an account on a dating site in my name that she'd been "checking out" for me. I immediately told her, "*No!*" Then, in case she decided to obey me for once in her life, I quickly added: "Well, are there any cute and rich guys out there?" I mean, if she was going shopping for me, she might as well search for the best product.

Maybe it wouldn't hurt to just look. Curious about what was involved in this new way of dating, I asked her questions: *How exactly does it work? What does it cost? Is it safe? What happens if you don't like any of the prospects? Is there any sort of book or manual that I need to read?*

Half of my daughter's lifetime ago, I had explained to her how dating at that time worked. Only my mother-daughter conversation dealt with the "Do Nots" and "Say Nos" when she was on a date. The "nots" and "nos" numbered a lot more than anything allowed.

Now the tables were turned, and I was getting the lecture. My daughter's explanation of dating electronically was full of technology words. Finally, exasperated at the blank stare I was giving her, she summed up by saying: "Trust me, Mom. It's very easy."

She offered to help me set up my own private account, and swore that if I didn't like it, she would discard my account on the site. I grudgingly decided to be brave and check it out. I had no idea what a strange, interesting, and intriguing world I was about to enter. Let me emphasize *strange*.

What to do? How does a person who hasn't dated for over forty years jump back in the dating pool? I tried to remember the rules that as a teen I had been given to follow. I never drank, smoked anything, or used bad language. I was the proverbial "good girl," mainly because I'd grown up hearing that I should never do anything I would not do if my mom were standing right behind me. Believe me, that thought kept me on the straight and narrow, even though there were plenty of temptations in the 1960s dating scene.

To think of dating some forty-odd years later was a bit scary. I could hardly remember what dating I'd done as a teenager with my then-future husband. What would it be like to date at this age? (Would I even *remember* any dates I got at this age?) Were the rules the same? Or had they changed as much in this century as hairdos had since the 1960s?

Curiosity got the better of me. The memory of how fun it had been to have turned back time for a few hours on my sixtieth birthday made me wonder if I would feel young again dating! That's how I ended up taking a road I'd never dreamed of traveling down.

Now that I've experienced dating through cyberspace, if someone were to ask me just how to join the Millennials in the dating world of today, I'd tell them two things: Watch every television show that features any type of dating, so that you're not constantly horrified by what people do nowadays; and keep in mind that you're *not* sixteen anymore.

Educational TV

I decided that if I were going to be dating in today's world, I wanted to be "with it," on par with twenty- or thirty-somethings, and up-to-date on how to hook a man, *if* I ever found one I thought was worth catching. There was *no* way I was going to ask my own children what they did on dates. I could Google "dating," but I'm more of a "picture is worth a thousand words" girl, so I turned to my old educational tool, the TV.

Television in the 1950s was quite tame compared to today's "bare all and bar none" attitude. There was no sex on any shows I remember from the 1950s. Lucy and Ricky slept in twin beds, Mr. and Mrs. Cleaver never entered a bedroom other than Wally and the Beav's, and *Bachelor Father* John Forsythe only had dinner dates.

By the time I was in my teens, television was starting to flirt with more adult-like shows. When *The Dating Game* first premiered in the late 1960s, the premise appeared to be a bit innocuous. A single young lady had a chance to choose one of three young men for a date, solely by asking questions of them. The catch was that she never saw them because they were seated behind a screen. Innocent enough until the questions and answers started becoming a bit risqué, with innuendos, and lots of laughter from the studio audience. I remember watching an episode where the contestant asked each of the three men what their favorite vegetable was. One answered green beans, but when the next man answered "big cucumbers," the girl giggled and the audience roared. Not being a veggie connoisseur and not liking the taste of anything remotely salad-y, I didn't understand what was so funny. I imagined at the time it was a ratings booster.

The television of today contains plenty of shows about dating. They're called sitcoms or reality shows, and while designed for entertainment, they can also be very educational. Before I let my daughter put me on the social network, I watched episodes of shows I'd never seen before, like *How I Met Your Mother*, *Sex and the City*, and *The Bachelorette*. In the interest of covering all bases, and to see what the *men* might be thinking, I even watched *The Bachelor*. Some of these shows made *The Dating Game* look as tame and innocent as the children's show of my generation *Captain Kangaroo*.

Whether it's for television ratings or the fact that the population of today is more sophisticated—or naughty— the shows of today leave little to the imagination in the world of romance and sex. Take for example, *The Bachelorette*. When a single lady, called a bachelorette, meets a group of eligible men, I was reminded of my college science class on mammalogy, specifically the part about mating rituals. The human males use their plumage, their grooming, and their physique to try to attract the female. And they do it in ways that would have earned censorship in the 1950s, but that seem to captivate the audience and raise ratings in the twenty-first century!

Sex and the City fascinated me. The fact that four beautiful young women could have sex with so many men, and then talk about their escapades as though they were reporting on something as common as getting their hair done, astounded me. I almost felt sorry for them, thinking that they had so many men instead of being able to find one true love. *Almost*, I said.

I didn't learn too much from these shows, except that the standard of good taste has gone south. But I did learn a whole new slew of words and phrases. The best way I can describe some of my new knowledge is to define what the words are *not*.

In the twenty-first century, "friends with benefits" does *not* mean someone with a swimming pool or a condo on the beach, or the person who orders an expensive, delicious dessert and then pushes it to you to eat. "Friends with benefits" has something to do with sex with someone you know but don't love. Evidently, the twenty-first century arrived without the lesson drilled into my parochial junior-high seventh-grade biology class from Sister Mary Andrew: "Sex is for procreation, *not* recreation."

In the dating world, "hook up" does *not* refer to what you do to your TV cable, a trailer, or your bra. I guess it can vary in its meaning to cover "hanging out" with a friend, talking with a stranger, or going at it like dogs in heat!

"DO ME" is *not* what kids beg when they want to be tossed up in the air, or have their fingernails painted like Mommy's. It's sexual. 'Nuff said.

Begin at the Beginning

Okay, at last I felt mentally and emotionally prepared for this new venture. I was also feeling skeptical. Would anyone even be interested in dating someone's grandmother?

When I mentioned to my friend JoAnn that I was letting my daughter put me on a dating site, and I wondered what was in store for me, she told me I was brave. The smile that lit up my face at this praise vanished as she continued: "If something happened to *my* husband, I'd never date or marry again. I would never let anyone else see me naked!"

NAKED! Eww. Yuck. I hadn't thought of that! It's one thing to have lived life's adventures with a mate and grown old together. It's quite another to realize that the defects on bodies that have aged through childbirth, day-to-day stress, and worry may be the trophies we've earned through those things, but aren't necessarily what we want to flaunt around to others. We both laughed.

"Oh, no! I'm all for beautifying America," I said, hastily. "That means *no* one sees me *au naturel*! Ever! I just want to find someone who can come over to the house if I need my mousetrap emptied."

"Hmm," she said, nodding. I nodded, too. I knew I was

not sixteen anymore. That meant my body was not young and supple, and my energy level was not as high as it once was. We stood silently for a minute. I'm sure we were picturing the same thing: overweight, middle-aged naked people. We both shuddered at the same time. I changed the subject and we talked about hair.

We should have kept the subject of "hair" to what's on our heads. Any other time of my life, hair would have been a safe subject. But God have mercy, most of us women over fifty are shaving more than just legs and underarms. (About the time the movie *The Lord of the Rings* appeared, my hair began sprouting in places it never had before, especially on the tops of my toes. Must have been hobbit contagion.) I could picture myself as a female Andy Rooney, with wild, untamed eyebrows and hair sprouting from my nose and chin. I expressed those fears, and was comforted by my neighbor's agreement and shared misery. We shuddered again.

"Well, what will you wear on a date?" Jo asked me. Good question. My wardrobe now consisted of business clothes for work, garden grubbies, and a variety of old jeans and T-shirts.

"Are tent dresses back in style?" I asked hopefully. Those would really cover a multitude of sins. We laughed again, and then parted ways.

I went home, opened my computer, and began shopping for tunic tops, jeans with Spandex, and shirts that covered up arm flags.

After a night of sleeping on the idea of dating after age sixty, I woke up thinking that this whole thing might be a waste of time, but at least I would be like the Baby Boomers of old—ready to try something new! So I said okay to my daughter, and with her patient help, I began my journey of online dating.

I was old—older, anyway. Which meant I was sometimes not as patient as I was thirty or forty years ago. I was under the mistaken impression that once I said I would try cyber-dating, all I had to do was turn on my computer. Nope.

What I learned about online dating is that it takes a lot of computer work. The first thing to do is open the free account. If your time is valuable, then scratch the "free" part. I swear this thing takes approximately fifty or sixty steps, and may even take up to a day or two. Once you're given an account, then you must fill out a profile, which does not mean you send in a side-view snapshot of yourself.

I'd heard that some dating sites had hundreds and hundreds of questions, ranging from standard physical ones (how tall are you?) to probing, insightful psychological ones (what five things can you not live without?). My site wasn't that hard, though. At least I *thought* it wasn't.

To begin, I had to come up with a "user name." There's no chance in the world you can simply use your first, last, or first and last name. That would be too easy. Plus, with what they call "hints" that pop up now and then, you're encouraged to be original, to be creative, to attract attention, and to choose a name you can *remember*.

The user name, or "handle," is supposed to be a way to stay anonymous, yet attract attention. I could only think of roadkill near a buzzard's nest. To come up with something interesting is hard. For us oldsters to try to remember what that interesting name *is* once it's selected, is harder. (I still have trouble recalling my password to get the garage door open when I forget to bring my automatic opener.)

I finally ended up using my initials and year of birth. The "creative" part was that instead of BBB, I used "TriB." After all, Delta Delta Delta sorority is easier said as "Tri-Delt," and if that abbreviation is good enough for college, it's good enough for me.

Next was the "catchphrase." Again, it should be something original and clever, but short and to the point—like a mission statement. Use of a quote or part of a song is also encouraged for those of us totally stymied by creating a statement that is not *Mission Impossible*.

Thinking I'd worn out my cleverness quota on the user name, I debated between two of my favorite quotes. One, from Groucho Marx, was "Man does not control his own fate. The women in his life do that for him." While that's true, I realized that probably over half the potential suitors out there were divorced for just that reason, so I nixed Mr. Marx.

I also loved one that has an anonymous author (probably because it's a universal observation). It reads: "Middle age is the time in your life when, after pulling in your stomach, you look as if you ought to pull in your stomach." That cracked me up. But while it certainly applied to me and a lot of other middle-aged people, it probably wasn't the best way to make a potential suitor eager to meet a paunchy, but funny, date.

I finally settled on another quote I loved, from Phyllis Diller: "A smile is a curve that sets everything straight." I hoped this journey would be straight going, and that I would have plenty to smile about.

Now for the parameters. How much of an age range was I going to allow these men to have? How far was I willing to travel to see someone?

Well, I definitely didn't want the men to be old enough I could claim them as my sugar daddies, and I didn't want them young enough that I could have been their mother! Maybe a little younger than me would not be so bad. I didn't want to mess with destiny and throw away the opportunity to meet Mr. Right just because I was the right age to be his big sister.

While a man would probably drive to meet me, I didn't want any stranger knowing where I lived at first. I picked thirty miles—that would cover driving to my favorite mall, which is where I planned to suggest to everyone we meet.

"Body Type" was next. I was dreading that one. If I'd thought I could diet and lose thirty pounds in a few months, like I *used* to be able to, I would have waited to sign up for this site. *I wonder if they levy a fine on members who lie on their profiles?* I thought. I looked at the choices of body types to see which one to check:

"Slender." *Maybe—if you look at my ankles.*

"Athletic and Toned." *Once upon a time.*

"Sexy." *Sexy? Is that a body type, or a look?*

I had to ponder this one. I'm one of those people who has probably never been thought of as being sexy. Nice, friendly, cute maybe . . . but not sexy. I *could* say I'm "stacked," but it's from the bottom up, not the top down. When I was in my thirties and *Flashdance* was popular, I once wore a sweatshirt of my husband's that hung off one shoulder. Maybe it was the strap of my Maidenform bra, or the fact that the sweatshirt front said: "If a man stands alone in the woods, and no one can hear him, is he still wrong?" but there was nothing sexy at all about it. You couldn't even make out my collarbone.

I so wanted to be able to put down that I was sexy, at least once in my life. But besides the sweatshirt incident, the only other "sexy" thing I'd tried on once had been a deep V-neck blouse that was supposed to seductively show some cleavage. When I'd stepped in front of the department store mirror to see myself, it had looked like I had a naked baby's butt stuck to my front.

End of pondering. I continued on for more body type choices:

"Chunky Monkey." *One of my favorite flavors of ice cream. No fair!*

"Big-Boned Babe." *It's not my bones that are big.*

"About Average." *Finally!* I thought of all the women I've ever seen. I was probably in between the skinny Minnies and the big-boned babes, so I guessed that made me about average. I went with this one.

"In Your Own Words." Only the few people in the

universe who actually enjoyed taking tests with essay questions in high school would love this part of the form. The site wanted you to write something about yourself and who you were looking for, and it had to be concise.

My mind went blank. Then a brilliant idea hit me. I'd check out the classified ads in the newspaper. There might be an ad for a woman seeking a man. Anyone who has to pay for an advertisement always makes it interesting, but concise. Surely there would be one I could use as a template.

I found only one good one:

Female, never had babies, loves to play. Especially loves sleeping on top of you or cuddled right next to your side. Also loves long walks and going hunting. Needs someone with energy and lots of love to give.

It was an ad for a dog.

I wasn't even through filling out this form, and already I was getting discouraged. One of the helpful little computer pop-ups offered tips on how to de-dullify your life and make it sound fantastic, and *yourself* desirable. There were even professional profilers who, for a small fee payable through a nationally accepted credit or debit card—or a mortgage on your home—would write your profile for you. I wished I'd seen that at the start.

The website encouraged me to post a recent picture of myself. The most recent picture of myself I had was my driver's license. I might as well have posted a mugshot. I'd never get a date with a driver's license photo! (I learned later that some people should probably look up the meaning of "recent" and try to control the urge to post their homecoming queen or football-player-of-the-week photo that's been tucked away for the past forty years.) My daughter found a photo of me holding my baby granddaughter in a way that covered my midsection, so I used that.

I was finally at the end of the beginning. All I needed to do was hit "Submit," sit back, and let the games begin. How long would I have to wait until my perfect match arrived?

It's Raining Men— Hallelujah?

The very next day, email popped up twenty-four matches for me. I swore I heard a "Ka-ching!" I'd hit the mother lode! *Twenty-four?* I thought. *Good grief—that's two dozen! It's positively raining men—hallelujah! Is the man I'm destined to meet going to be there? Is he tall? Handsome? Twinkling eyes? How can I possibly be able to pick* one *from so many at once? And this is only Day One.* I tried to think of a gift to send to my daughter as a finder's fee.

In a second, the images appeared, and a millisecond later the mother lode yielded fool's gold. Yes, there were two dozen images, but of what? None of these looked like my teen idol David Cassidy—then *or* now. Where were the handsome models from the television ads? Had I made a mistake and put a "1" in front of the age parameters? These guys looked positively ancient!

Time and memory can sometimes be like oil and water—they don't mix. The last time I'd been on the dating scene was in the late 1960s. Potential dates then had heads of shaggy or wavy hair, full muttonchops (or scraggly facsimiles thereof), shining eyes, youthful sexiness in their smiles and grins, and complexions that showed both the young children they had been such a short time ago and the hint of the young men they were about to become.

The profile pictures I saw in that first batch sported heads in various stages of baldness and/or gray hair. Jowls replaced youth's muscular clean lines; some were covered in various wispy beards. Their eyes were shiny, but I think that was from the glare on their glasses. I was looking at a bunch of men, my fellow Baby Boomers, my peers in the aging process, and it took me quite a few minutes to get my bearings and rearrange my expectations of what I could find online in the way of dates. Nope, we *definitely* were not sixteen anymore.

There were a variety of pictures. The photos ranged from deer-in-the-headlights looks to suave and sophisticated. A few had submitted good quality, professional-looking pictures. Some were fuzzy and grainy. Some were snapshots taken with a grandchild blocking part of the man's features. (I was not alone!)

It's a strange phenomenon that once we get to a certain age, and/or have children and grandchildren, we don't have too many pictures of ourselves alone. It might be because we can't figure out how to take selfies. But chances are it's just that the younger generation is so cute and precious, we can't take enough pictures of them.

It shouldn't have come as any surprise that quite a few of these people only had pictures of themselves that were obviously cropped because they had been taken on special occasions that included a group. There was the guy in a tuxedo, a big grin on his face, holding a bottle of beer aloft and bent over toward a sliver of someone in a silvery gown, who presumably was also happy—at least at that time, if it was a former wife.

There was another man who looked, at first glance, like he had a lot of hair. A second glance revealed that his mane was really the locks of some long-haired brunette, whose face and torso had been clipped out of his photo—and probably out of his life.

One of the cropped photos made me grab my magnifying glass. Yes. That was definitely a tongue coming from the side of oblivion and licking this guy's cheek. It must have been a dog, because it was certainly the longest and skinniest tongue I'd ever seen. Just in case it wasn't, though, I made a mental note to skip this man. I wasn't sure I was ready to be someone's new "pet."

Finally, there were those without any picture at all. Either they had no concept of how to download a photo, or they were hiding something. These guys needed to get with the computer technology available today and do what I had to do to download my pictures: call a child to help out.

Profiles in Courage?

Well, it was now or never. I clicked on the first match. This was amazing. The computer assured me by message just what I had in common with this potential date. So we wouldn't feel like total strangers, I assumed. Yes, we were definite matches—on two things. We "Like Kids"...and... we "Each Have a Dog." Well, then I matched ninety-nine percent of my granddaughter's preschool class.

But I was committed to this now, so I continued to read the first match's profile. Then I moved to the second, third, and finally made it through all twenty-four. It was like surfing the channels on TV—nothing to watch!

Could I be so out of touch with the single males my age? I was hoping to find someone who wanted to go to the movies, or out for ice cream, or who loved Coney dogs and A&W Root Beer at the outside drive-in. A majority of the twenty-four matches had an undercurrent of sexual tension in them. If youth had forsaken these guys' looks, it appeared to be alive and kicking in their graphic yearnings for a mate.

Some of their descriptions of what kind of woman they were looking for, and what their ideal date with said woman would be like, could have gone into a soft-porn magazine. I know men think differently, but for heaven's sake! It was like being around a bunch of prairie chickens, puffing and strutting their stuff, thinking they were enticing an unknown pool of females with their romantic prowess and their ability to delight their ladylove(s). There was even one motorcycle-obsessed dude who pointed out that his dates could put their arms around his waist—or wherever the ladies were more comfortable hanging on (wink, wink)—as they rode off together to experience who knows what. Oh, and I almost forgot: they all had a good sense of humor, according to their collective profiles. I think their dates were going to need that.

I also learned one of my first lessons about social networking: "Don't always believe what you see." I soon realized that some guys tended to put their best-looking picture on their main page, no matter how young they were in the photo.

Ah, but hope springs eternal, right? The next day a whole new batch of matches appeared. Well, there was something to be said for having the ego stroked every day. The sixteen-year-old inside of me actually felt a little popular!

This batch had *some* nice-looking men. There were actually a few I wanted to check out, maybe not to date, but rather because some of them looked unbelievable.

"LUVNFUNIN69" at least had a better-quality picture than most. But the poor guy must have had too much fun and not enough love in 1969; he looked like he'd been dragged through the wringer once or twice. He had a gaunt face. At least, I *thought* it was gaunt, but I really couldn't tell for sure because of all the hair he had. He had long gray hair, a long gray beard and mustache, and eyebrows that looked more like a Fu Manchu. I think they actually connected down to his mustache. Maybe he used to play for ZZ Top, or was on *Duck Dynasty*. Or maybe he'd come here to Iowa from Hollywood, where he was a character actor. He certainly *looked* like a character. His catchphrase was: "I'd like a shot at you." That certainly sent my heart racing, but not in a good way.

One memorable one was "PLZBMIME." I thought at first that was a typo, and that it was a cute Valentine-y way to say "please be mine." His main photo was of a rather young-looking man in a trench coat. "Young-looking" and "sixty" don't mesh, so I quickly looked through the three other pictures that were attached to the profile page. Aha! There was a definite reason for his "typo." It was there, in stark black-and-white-faced makeup: a very professionally done portrait of a real-life mime, complete with black-and-white striped shirt, black suspenders, and a black hat. Good heavens! If a man showed up to a date dressed like that, what on earth would I talk about? And what kind of makeup did he use that must have kept his skin looking young?

I read his profile. He was obviously one of those passion-filled romanticists, and a bit like the horny men in my first batch of profiles. He wrote, in a Harlequin novel-esque way, of what his ideal date would be for the woman lucky enough to connect with him. First, they'd fly to Seattle, Washington, and hop aboard a train. That train ran to the East through parts of Canada and the United States. It would stop in St. John, Maine, near the Bay of Fundy (that's a real place—I checked!) There, on a hilltop covered in grass, Mime and his lady would make mad, passionate love.

All this on a first date? Oh, brother, give me a break! All I could picture was dry grass sticking to the white face paint. I wondered what kind of passionate declarations of love could come out of the throat of a silent mime in the midst of the sexual throes of ecstasy. I don't think there's ever been a Harlequin novel that has addressed an image that hideous!

But just so I didn't think PLZBMIME was so horribly odd, "BEESBMYN" popped up a few days later. Maybe we were a match because we each had at least one "B" in our call name. Beezy was listed as "Never Married" in the relationship part—and I saw why. His profile said he'd just gotten over a five-year relationship with a woman. I thought there might be several reasons why he'd never made it down matrimony lane. For one thing, he was looking strictly for blondes (note the plural form he used) . . . blondes who loved to be surprised. (Wait till they saw his profile picture!)

Poor Beezy—he evidently didn't know how to surprise the ladies, because his profile picture left little to the imagination. There he was—splayed over a sofa wearing what looked like adult "Underoos." My kids had had

Underoos when they were getting potty-trained. They were matching undies and T-shirts, some with little characters on both the top and bottom, and some in matching pastel colors.

Beezy's looked like they'd once been white, but had been washed with a bunch of dirty jeans, because they were almost a putty color—certainly not a sexy color. His pose looked as though Beezy was trying to present a provocative, "come-hither, maidens" look, a la George Costanza in a *Seinfeld* episode. . . except George looked way better.

Some of these people couldn't be for real. Maybe some of these "dates" were actually victims of practical jokes. I decided that had to be the case. At least I hoped so.

But I plowed on. Each day, either I was getting more desperate to find a real match, or the candidates were actually getting better.

And after a few days . . .

BINGO!

First Crush

It's one thing to be able to look through batches of potential suitors anonymously. It's another to actually make contact with one—or several, as the case may be. What would I do if someone wanted to meet me? Or worse, what would I do if I was interested in meeting someone whose profile looked appealing?

As soon as I'd agreed to do electronic dating, I had started worrying about that. I finally decided I would take my time before actually meeting anyone face-to-face. Emailing would be safe, and I could edit and proof my mail before I sent it in order to make sure I impressed my potential suitors—if I wanted to. This way, I figured, we'd know each other better so we'd know whether to finally go on a date.

The first invitation I got to meet was a test of my plan. His profile picture was a headshot of a man with lots of wavy, white hair. It was long enough that it looked a little carefree, but short enough that it wasn't unkempt. He wore rimless glasses that made him look bookishly intelligent. I wondered if he was a teacher. He wanted to meet me to go for a walk around the city lake. He looked harmless enough, and certainly nice, but . . . I imagined a dark alley, a robbery, or worse. I asked if he'd mind emailing a bit first, and to my delighted surprise, he agreed!

His emails were to the point, brief, but very interesting. I soon learned he was a retired newspaper reporter. Aha! He'd learned to adhere to spatial parameters in his writing career, and he obviously liked news. I carefully crafted my emails to him, trying to match his interests, while staying as concise as possible.

I failed. After trying to cram thoughts and feelings into a short sentence, I gave up and figured he could edit them himself. *I am who I am*, I told myself, *and I like to talk, even if it's only through cyberspace.* Each email I wrote to him was full of interesting tidbits, but I was careful not to reveal too much—otherwise, what would I have to say verbally if we ever met face-to-face?

I also tried to make sure I came across as a caring, thoughtful woman, but not the smothering, mothering type I'd heard men so dreaded. I botched that, too.

When my "Roving Reporter" mentioned he'd ridden a bike, hit a mud puddle, and spattered mud up the back of his shirt, unfortunately the mom in me told him he should immediately soak his shirt in detergent first and rinse it. I finished my missive with a dissertation on how to whiten whites. Smothering? I practically asphyxiated him with my concern. I also let him know I was amused at his predicament (lots of LOLs and happy-face emoticons) and subtly praised him for that kind of exercise at his age

("Wow! You still ride a bike? That's great!") I was positive I was intriguing him.

After several days, and many emails, at last I felt comfortable enough to tell him my name. He wrote back, succinctly, of course: "Becky—nice name." *Oh! He likes me!*

What I read into those three words would fill a steamy set of narratives. I was hooked on this whole electronic dating thing. He wouldn't have given me that tiny, insignificant compliment if he wasn't really interested in me, right? I decided to let Fate take its course and casually emailed him a suggestion that we finally meet in person, and . . . GLITCH! At least that's how he put it. I felt "crushed" over my first "crush."

Evidently while I was taking my time, thinking I was winning him over, another female match for him had totally skipped the email part by meeting face-to-face, which ultimately led to another date, and another, which led him to tell me he didn't want to juggle two people.

Okay. My first experience of electronic dating excitement shorted out. But I absorbed that escape excuse of not wanting to juggle. Everyone can relate to that. *May have to use that someday*, I thought. *Lesson learned. Nice touch. Like it.*

First Date—Kinda

After learning that emailing can equate to snail mailing or just plain bombing out, I got an email from one of my contacts, asking me if we could meet for coffee sometime. Since I had tried emailing two other men recently and struck out (no replies!), I was ready to try something else. What could I say to this guy?

"Yes!" I'm sure he heard my answer from miles away before I emailed him. I wondered if I'd have enough days before we met to drop those ten or twenty pounds I'd been meaning to drop. *Must get a new outfit. Wish my nails weren't so short and that my fingers weren't so stubby. And how fast can I firm up my neck?*

In the next few minutes, he emailed, notifying me he had to run to a lumberyard first, but he could meet me in an hour. *Whoa! This guy means business. Wow.* Wait! *An hour? Oh, good grief. No way.*

It was Saturday morning, and I already had a date—with my garage. I had gotten up extra early to beat the heat and had been sweeping the filthy floor, tossing old dog bones and broken flower pots, and getting downright dirty with all the other junk I was trying to throw away.

No makeup, hadn't even taken a shower. The only reason I had known about this email was that I'd come in to take a quick break. I should have kept the computer turned off!

Give me two hours, I emailed him back. Done. We had a date. I had a DATE! My first one in over forty years.

I also had exactly an hour and a half before I met him at a bookstore a half hour away. I raced to the shower, shedding dusty, smelly clothes as I went. My panic subsided under the warm water, and I almost took my time shampooing and rinsing my hair. This short notice was really a blessing in disguise. I'm one of those people who, if I had made the date for the next day, would have spent twenty-four hours and a sleepless night worrying about what to wear, what to say, and what emergency provisions (as in breath spray, perfume, hair spray, spare contact lenses, and whatever else I could think of) I should pack for my date.

With no time to spare, I managed to get cleaned up, dressed, and primped. And there I was, speeding to the mall, until I started thinking about what I was really about to do. I managed to calm down my nerves and drove to our meeting destination: a nice, safe bookstore with a coffee shop in a huge shopping mall.

I arrived. Early, even. I wondered if he was already in the bookstore, and if so, if maybe he was looking out the window and watching me! Just in case he was, I walked slowly, with just a hint of a feminine swing in my hips that I hoped wouldn't be mistaken for a limp. It was sunny, which sometimes causes me to squint and frown, so I composed my face into a little close-mouthed smile. *Yeah!*

Slight smile to show how approachable I am. Plus it'll do wonders to pull those lines above my lips apart.

But it was all for naught—he wasn't there yet. I had arrived too early. Now I had time to worry. *What do I do? How do I kill time? Do I prowl the bookshelves and look intellectual before he comes? Do I grab a seat in the coffee area and hope the baristas don't ask me to leave? How do I greet this guy? A businesslike handshake? A wave? A hug? What do I do? Someone tell me, quickly.*

The shop was starting to fill up, so I ordered a diet pop and grabbed a table. After a few minutes, I realized that the chairs were probably designed to encourage people to chug their drinks and leave. It felt like I was sitting on cement. *Yikes! What if my bursitis acts up? If I want to impress this guy, will he be turned off as soon as I stand up and hobble away?*

I didn't get much chance to dwell on that, because I finally spotted him. He was one of the men who had a very nice-looking profile picture, and he looked just like it. Thinning blond and gray hair, a genuine smile, and glasses made him look nice and friendly. But I could tell he was definitely more nervous than I was, which calmed me down immensely. He also looked *older* than I'd thought he was, when he was really four years younger than I.

We shook hands shyly, and he asked me if I would like anything to drink or eat. *Hmm,* I thought, *one point for very nice manners.* I declined, pointing at my large pop, so he got himself an iced tea. When he was back, we settled down to talk. Well, *I* settled down to talk.

There had recently been a segment on a national television station: "How Long Is Too Long a Silence in a Conversation?" A study found that four seconds was the breaking point—by four seconds of lagging conversation, someone always breaks the silence. I sure didn't need that study to know when to feel awkward.

I talked for a bit, then politely paused so he could have his turn. Either this guy was so enthralled with me that he was rendered speechless, or else he had absolutely nothing to say. I assumed the former. He was certainly a good listener, I'll grant him that. But when I paused, he just kept smiling at me and remained silent. I would count: *One, one thousand, two, one thousand, three, one thousand,* and I would break and start talking again . . . and again.

I drained my large Diet Coke in no time, and soon my throat was parched and my voice was raspy. I told him about my childhood, my childrens' childhood, and my grandchildrens' childhood. Since my grandchildren were only three years, two years, and six months old, that part didn't take up much time. I named every pet I'd ever owned, and all the schools I ever attended. I even debated—*with myself*—the pros and cons of parochial school versus public school, as he silently nodded in agreement. I *did* ask him a couple of questions every once in awhile, but the most he ever answered was about a sentence or two.

And then silence. I'd glance around at nearby book titles to see if there was anything else we—or I—could talk about. He gazed off into the distance, and *one, one thousand, two, one thousand, three, one thousand* . . . I broke into his reverie and started talking. Maybe the poor guy was finally trying to gather his thoughts and might have possibly expounded upon something, but I just wasn't able to give him a four-second chance.

About the time the large Diet Coke had followed its gastric journey and I wished I hadn't drunk it, I realized I couldn't stand the sound of my own voice any longer. Obviously, this date was boring, and we were not a match. I love conversation, not lecturing.

I finally stood up, told him goodbye by shaking hands again, and automatically said that I'd enjoyed meeting him, but didn't think there was any chemistry between us. I wished him luck. He seemed a bit startled at that, but kept smiling, said okay, and good luck, too, and he thanked me.

I headed back home to my unclean garage. But at least I felt I'd broken the ice on my widowhood. I was now, officially, a single person who was dating. It may not have gone the way I imagined a date would go, but I could look on the bright side: my first date had been with a *younger* man.

Woo-hoo! The old gal still had it! Did that make me a cougar? It was scary, exhilarating, and puzzling at the same time, but I was hooked. *This might actually prove to be fun*, I thought.

Urges

I have to confess that I soon became secretly thrilled to be on the electronic dating circuit. I have always admired people who are independent, strong, and able to grasp life and get everything out of it they want without needing anyone or any help. I am not one of those wonderful beings. I was chicken—and I didn't realize it at first. The thought of having someone else to talk to besides my dog Ralphie, and getting to mix and mingle with friends as part of another couple, instead of being a "fifth wheel," was intoxicating. I felt happy. But there appeared to be other feelings.

Suddenly being thrust into the world of dating, especially since I had not been with a man for quite a number of years, can be a shock to a woman's system. Not only was I scoping out every single man who came across my computer, but suddenly every individual stranger I happened to see in day-to-day circumstances became an object to scrutinize, just to see if he could possibly be the one.

I believe it is only natural that the huntress seeks to be the hunted—and with the thrill of the chase, there awakens innate urges: urges as old as Eve, when she bit into a strawberry and its juice stained her lips (the Garden had more than mere apples, you know, and someone had to invent lipstick!).

Of course, I'm talking about that urge we women get that can cause shudders to ripple through the body, cause the breath to come in gasps, and that can actually physically hurt when it's not satisfied. It is the urge . . . to shop for oneself.

I hadn't felt that urge for decades. I was dating. I needed to get some new things, and not from the Internet. I didn't have to shop for my kids, my dog, my relatives . . . just for me! Heaven help me, it was an almost sinful feeling to experience so much pleasure when that fact sunk in. Woo-hoo!

Makeup, hair color, new clothes, shoes, glasses, contacts—whatever tripped my trigger, I gave in to it. Only once did my conscience bother me. I spent almost one hundred dollars on a face cream that promised to make my old-age spots disappear. But I could justify that. I just wouldn't buy a new supply of Cadbury Eggs next Easter season. Yes, it was pathetic, I know, but I could save a hundred dollars giving up those addictive sweets.

I even became obsessed with Spanx. The notion that you can have your cake and eat it too, and look slim just by putting on Spanx, was too much of a temptation. Like a bricklayer at the base of the Dubai Towers, I set out to make my foundation as solid and supportive as possible. I was now the proud owner of an assortment of Spanx that addressed the same parts of my body as the picture of cuts of beef did at the local locker. I had Spanx that accentuated my calves, trimmed my thighs, made my muffin-tops delectable, and made my "girls" proud! I was amazed at how versatile Spanx was: bust, butt, waist, hips, back, and front, there was something for every part of my body. That was, except my turkey-wattle neck, but I could throw a scarf around that!

Those extra-small, designer-brand dresses wouldn't be any problem to slip into now. My muffin-top was actually cinched in to form a "natural" waist. My sagging glutes formed a round, apple-like little butt, and my chest . . . well, no one would ever again be able to crack jokes about my bosoms knocking against my knees.

I even planned to get all new underwear! No more granny panties. No XXL cheap sports bras. No hiding the varicose veins under elastic-waist stretch pants. I would be able to wear real pantyhose. Just thinking of how I would look made me feel thirty years younger. Whoever my next date was going to be, I pitied him. I thought:

Mama's feelin' frisky!

Cheesecake Fiasco

My second date was with a gentleman who had sent me an email noting he liked my smile and that I was a beautiful lady. Compliments will get me every time!

But since I had at least three other emails going on, I sent him a guilt-stricken email back that I wasn't educated enough in the etiquette of technological dating. I was afraid I'd bitten off more than I could chew with all the correspondence I was having, and would he mind if I contacted him at a later date? He was happy that I might be available, and contented to delay meeting. I couldn't help but be flattered that he was willing to wait for me. His emails to me had been chatty, sweet, with no sexual undertone, and were just plain charming.

Soon after I gave up on the two poor souls I'd probably bored to death with my emails, I got an email from him just asking how I was doing. This came the day after my half-silent first date. I had regained my voice, so his timing was good. The next morning, on a Monday, I emailed him that if he was still interested in meeting sometime, I'd be available!

In the middle of the afternoon, he emailed me to see

if I'd meet him at The Cheesecake Factory at a local mall that evening. *The Cheesecake Factory? I thought. Yumm-OH! Hooray! Wait. This evening? Three hours after I get off work? Oh, no, another quick-get-ready date.* If this was how dates were going to be all the time, I was going to have to learn how to assemble some sort of method to get ready quickly. How did runway models change so fast? Better find out.

I wondered: Was striking quickly a secret tip from dating sites for gentlemen, in order for them to be able to catch ladies and see our true colors? Did they not realize what it's like to try to date when you're in menopause? It's a wonder I didn't snap the heads off of these last-minute daters. I wondered if my user name should have been "PrayingMantis," or "BlackWidow." I considered putting in my profile that I required a twenty-four-hour minimum notice before a date, especially one involving a dinner.

If I'd known ahead of time, I wouldn't have eaten lunch, so I could truly enjoy *cheesecake*. Speaking of time, didn't men realize how long it takes for a woman to cream, wax, shave, pluck, dye, straighten, curl, buff, polish, spray, brush, whiten, tan, gargle, and practice smiling? That's not even allowing time for choosing what to wear: slacks, shorts, skirt, dress, elastic waist, belt, shoes, sandals, boots, short-sleeved, long-sleeved, sleeveless (no, not sleeveless with *my* triceps!), jacket, sweater, jewelry or not?

One close look in the mirror, and I thought: *Oh. My. GAWD! Makeup—eek! Where'd my eyebrows go? When did that cute little sprinkling of freckles turn into age spots? Have they created lipstick that stays on your lips, not on your teeth, yet? Speaking of lips, why are mine the only skinny part of my entire body? Aww, what the heck. Since beauty is in the eye of the beholder, I'll just hope we go somewhere dark. Is Cheesecake Factory dark? Wear the elastic waistband, right?*

My first date had been a good practice run for how to look relatively ravishing in sixty minutes or less. I got to the mall fifteen minutes before my seven p.m. Cheesecake Factory date was to begin. Worried that my hair might have frizzed in the heat and humidity of an Iowa summer as soon as I got out of the car, I rushed to the restroom near the food court.

I spent a few minutes trying to make my approximately inch-and-a-half-long hair longer in order to cover the "chub" but leave the "bones" showing in my cheeks, so that I'd look slender—at least in my face. Hair doesn't stretch. I couldn't eat with my cheeks sucked in, anyway, so I gave that up. I psyched myself up and strode out into the mall, sucking in the one thing I could—my stomach.

I was confident, radiant, self-assured, and ready to meet my date. I found a chair at the far end of the food court across from the entrance to Cheesecake Heaven—I mean Factory. It was a *great* vantage point. I could also see both the west and south entrances to the mall from there. Then I began to look for my date. It was exactly seven p.m.

Suddenly, there seemed to be lots of single men walking by. Maybe they were looking for their wives. Maybe one was looking for me. I was careful not to frown as I squinted my eyes, trying to see if one of them was *the one*. I decided I definitely should make an appointment with my eye doctor to strengthen my contact lenses.

As I studied each male and mentally checked off the ones who didn't fit my date's picture, I wondered just how true his photo had been. Maybe I couldn't tell from his picture what he looked like. Maybe he was really tall . . . maybe super handsome . . .

Then I saw him and gasped.

Coming in my direction was a man with a smile on his face, and about the same height and build as the picture on the dating site. Except this bozo was wearing a *Cat in the Hat* hat.

Oh, dear God, no, I prayed. *This must be some sort of joke. How fast can I politely eat supper and get out of here? Maybe he won't see me*. But he was headed right toward me dead-on.

I screwed up my courage, reminded myself not to judge a book by its cover, held my breath, and smiled, painfully, at him . . . but he was looking straight ahead and walked on by. If anyone had been standing in front of me, they would have been blown backward from all the air I expelled in relief. False alarm, thank heaven. I couldn't see filling in conversational voids with a man whose hat I'd have been staring at all night.

Well, then where was my date? You'd think if he was in such an all-fired hurry to make a date, he'd have been here early, too. I called my daughter Brooke, the matchmaker, who pointed out it was only five minutes past seven.

Why didn't I call him, she asked? Because, uh, I hadn't even thought to ask for a phone number. I couldn't even call Cheesecake Factory to see if there were reservations, because I didn't have his last name. He was just "Dave." Lesson learned, another of the very many I had a feeling were waiting to be acquired.

Five minutes later, I called my other daughter, Alyssa, who lived on the West Coast. She suggested I walk into Cheesecake Factory to see if he was sitting inside on the bench by the door to the mall. I hurried over to the entrance, opened the door, and . . . nobody there.

Another ten minutes crept by. I called Brooke again to have her go on my email account and see if he had emailed me he would be late.

"Nothing there," she reported. "Have you gone inside?"

"Yes," I sighed. "No one was on that bench by the restrooms."

"Did you check the other entrance?" she asked.

"*Other* entrance? What other entrance?"

"The one next to the reservation booth," she said, sounding more like my mother than my child.

What reservation booth? With my cell stuck to my ear, my daughter guided me verbally through what I thought had been the only entrance, told me to keep on going and make a right turn where I'd find—yup! There was my poor date, sitting hunched over his knees on a bench at the *other* entrance, looking so dejected!

He looked up and immediately smiled at me—with a hint of relief, I thought! I was so embarrassed, but we shook hands, confessing we'd each thought we'd been stood up.

We ended up having a very lovely dinner, dessert (of course), and conversation. He was just like his emails: very sweet, a true gentleman, and fun to talk to. I felt like I had found a new friend, although I didn't think there were any romantic sparks. And I was very glad I had worn the elastic waistband.

It's Baseball Season—Errors Galore and Someone Just Stole First Base

I'd had several weeks of emails from a man whose online photo reminded me of former University of Iowa football coach Hayden Fry. Since he lived over two hours away, I'd dismissed his profile. But evidently two hours from me wasn't too much for him. He emailed me a few days after my Cheesecake Factory date and wanted to meet me, any place that I chose. There was a little niggling voice in the back of my head that said: *What if he got all the way down here and you don't like him? How would you get rid of him?* In an inspired move, I emailed him that I would meet him in a city that was almost halfway between us, and I'd let him know the exact location soon.

I Googled places to go and decided that since a shopping mall had worked for the first two dates, I would pick one in the area that was nice and populated. That way, I could hightail it out of there if the date was going to be a bust.

While I was in the midst of Googling, my next-door

neighbor, Joyce, stopped over with her adorable little two-year-old granddaughter. She invited me to come over to her house, and since I love babies and toddlers, I promised I would after I finished setting up the date on the computer.

Then Brooke called. I told her about my plans to visit Joyce and her grandbaby. I also told her the good news that I had a new date.

"Wow, Mom! A date with three different guys in one week?" She was either duly impressed, or truly shocked that her old mom was this busy. I felt a little embarrassed. And a teensy bit proud.

I mentioned to her that I needed to cut the phone call short in order to send an email to this man. She started to say, "Remember . . . " but I anticipated her instructions and promised her I would get his phone number (lesson learned from the Cheesecake Factory fiasco). I'd give him mine, too. Brooke just laughed, and we hung up.

Keep in mind there are only so many little grey cells in one's brain. A sixty-one-year-old brain has even fewer, especially if it's continually bombarded by chemicals from assorted shades of blonde from Miss Clairol. I emailed my date the information of where and when to meet, gave him my phone number, and asked him for his. Then I ran next door for some baby time!

Not too long after I was there, Joyce's phone rang. It was my daughter calling for me.

Naturally, I thought one of her kids was sick, but she immediately questioned me in a singsong voice: "Guess who I just talked to? Your date for this Saturday."

I was totally confused. My first thought was: *Oh my God, is he stalking me? How did he know to call my daughter? Is he checking up on me? What is going on?*

My child was laughing her head off! It seemed her dyed-in-the-brain blonde mother had hastily typed *her* (my daughter's) cell number in the email to the guy, and he had called it to give *me* his phone number. He was certainly as confused as I was!

To cover my embarrassment, I whined to my daughter, "C'mon! Who really knows their own cell phone number?" In reality, I even need to check my cell phone's menu to dial 9-1-1!

My self-appointed personal dating guru Brooke advised me to give the man a call right away. I ran back home and phoned him. Thank heaven he seemed to have a sense of humor. He just wanted to double-check where this mall was located; he didn't Google much, he admitted. He was chuckling because he told me my daughter had told him that he needed to notice from my profile picture that I actually *was* blonde. (I know there are all sorts of terrible "isms" out there, like racism and sexism—is there one against a certain hair color?)

We made a date for mid-morning Saturday at the mall, about an hour away. Crisis averted. And I liked the sound of his voice!

Saturday arrived. I got there first, of course, and did some window shopping before my cell suddenly rang. My date had arrived and was in the parking lot. I stepped outside the mall, and . . . I swore I could hear Jimmy Dean singing the song "Big Bad John." My grandmother had had that record, and when I was little, I had always tried to picture a guy standing six foot six and weighing 245 pounds! Well, there stood my childhood fantasy in person. I hoped my jaw hadn't dropped open.

My date was *huge*! Certifiably six foot six, as the song said, and if not "narrah" at the hip, he certainly wasn't bad-looking. I was a little nervous and intimidated by his height. As I craned my neck to look up at him, I thought that if this giant called me "Gidget," I'd punch him in the kneecap! But he was very nice. We shook hams, I mean, *hands*, and then we wandered into the mall.

During the next few hours of our date, I called him "Dave" three times. That was *not* his name. Dave had been the name of my Cheesecake Factory date. I guess I was still impressed with the cheesecake! After the phone number mix-up, I didn't want "Big Bad John" to think I was a total idiot who couldn't get his name straight. So I laughed each time and blamed my calling him Dave on the fact that right before he drove into the parking lot, I'd just gotten off the phone with my brother, Dave. And yes, my nose grew each time with that lie. Duh.

Big Bad John was a slow talker, but we covered a variety of topics: from George Washington Carver, to the price of farmland, to, finally, some nitty-gritty stuff. Such as he'd dated some crazy women who immediately tried to shed their clothes when they first met him.

Oohh-kay. I wasn't quite sure how I was to react to that news. Was I supposed to be impressed? Was he bragging? I really didn't know. What I started thinking, however, was that he must be a ladies' man. He always seemed to be looking at other women, even while talking to me, his date. Maybe it was because his eyes were up so high that he could see more. Maybe it was because he was so tall that he attracted the attention of a lot of people, especially women. Whatever, it was a turn-off for me. I decided to go with my gut instinct and figure out how soon I could get away and go home.

Eventually Big Bad John suggested we try one of the mall restaurants. After we were seated, he excused himself for a minute, and I seized the opportunity to call Brooke. I told her to call me in one hour, figuring that would give me time to eat and kind of segue out of there.

But I soon found that when we were seated, all of Big Bad John's attention was on me. And when the topic of conversation suddenly changed from football teams and farming to *me*, by golly, the time flew by!

By the time my daughter called, I was only halfway done with my taco salad and my story about why I love Tom Bergeron on *Dancing with the Stars*. I figured I'd better go, though. I told her in a loud voice, while she giggled on the other end, that I would be *glad* to help her with the kids, and I could be at her place in an hour and a half or so.

"Well, I'd better get going, Da . . . uh . . . " I tried to sound halfway remorseful. I didn't want to hurt this man's feelings, even though I was sure we'd probably never meet again. He lived too far away, I thought.

He gave me a knowing grin, and asked, "Was that your escape call?"

Busted! Jeepers! Was his hearing range a lot bigger than average, too? Obviously he was a more experienced dater than I and had used that ploy himself, or another date had used it on him before. Of course, I lied and denied it and told him I was *so* sorry to have to leave. He just grinned.

Well, Big Bad John did have a streak of decency. He was very gentlemanly, and walked me to my car. I was debating how to shake hands—a straight arm thrust across my body to his right hand, a warm clasp with two hands since, after all, he'd just bought me a meal, or just a casual wave and a "Thanks for lunch and drive safely"? Or did I give him a sisterly little hug at the waist, which was as high as I could reach, which meant I'd be eye-to-navel with him? Eeek.

Well, he took care of my indecisiveness. He bent about three of his six and a half feet, wrapped me in a bear hug, and planted a kiss right on my mouth. And it wasn't just a quick little peck. I stepped back, patted his arm, and said, brilliantly, "Oh."

I hadn't seen that coming. What did I do now? Were senior citizens allowed to get to *first base*? My mind was reeling. I had just been *kissed*. Should I really leave him with that shocked "Oh?"

As I climbed in my car and he shut my door for me, I racked my brain for a better way to say goodbye than "oh." I guess part of his earlier conversation had stuck with me, because I blurted out: "Well, you can tell your kids *I* kept my clothes on."

Big Bad John just looked down at me and gave me another little grin.

I was desperately wishing someone would *please* write a manual of "things to say that don't sound dumb." I sincerely doubted I'd see him again. I didn't know how my face got sunburned from being inside the mall, but my cheeks were still burning an hour after I drove home. I decided: *I've either gotta quit this dating game already, start dating only guys named Dave, or find Mr. Right soon.*

When I got home, I opened up Facebook and asked:

Does anybody know a sweet David Cassidy or Hugh Jackman look-alike with a sense of humor (and a big bank account), preferably never-before-married because presumably he's spent his whole life looking for a sixty-one-year old klutz?

There were no answers.

Pucker Up, Baby

Big Bad John's kiss had been my first "date kiss" in decades. I couldn't get it out of my mind. As a matter of fact, I thought about it so much, I'm afraid I became a little obsessed about it. I had no idea how I was going to get through dating at this age, when a mere kiss could make such an impression on me.

I come from a family of kissers. In my family, affection and love are shown in a multitude of ways—winks, hugs, pats, pet names, teasing, smiles—but kissing is our preferred method. My parents always kissed me on the lips. I kiss my children on the lips, my grandbabies on the lips, and once—I stress this was wholly unintentional and accidental—I got a kiss on the mouth from my dog! (He was after the peanut butter I hadn't had time to wipe from my face.)

Lips were meant to be kissed. When I was sixteen, I learned that boys who would never be seen even holding hands in public seemed to know about lip kissing—as long as it was in the confines of a parked car at the drive-in, hidden in the darkness of night, or stolen inside the safe boundaries of a building. Kissing a girl on the lips was practically considered a feather in the cap of young manhood. Kissing was not only a sign of affection, but it was—and is—enjoyable!

There is a summer tradition in my hometown that I always look forward to, and that is my annual reunion with dear hometown friends at the town's sweet corn festival. I always get my "kiss fix" at that time. There are a couple of my male friends who demonstrate our platonic affection by kissing a bunch of us "girls" on the lips, no matter how old we all are. They do this in front of their wives, who just so happen to also be in a line to get bussed by someone else! It's all part of our affection connection as older people. I love these dear hearts and gentle people who let me know that I'm loved, not only by my family, but my friends.

Was this first kiss from "Big Bad John" a sign of affection? Or purely platonic, like from my friends? If I ever saw him again, would he even *want* to kiss me? I started dissecting every thought I had about that. Why was I, a mature woman who had lived for over seven decades, getting her mind warped by one simple little kiss?

I'm pretty good at arguing with myself, playing devil's advocate. I had also become quite dependent on Google. I Googled pros and cons of a "kiss on a first date." The word "player" was listed in the cons, and so I had to look it up. The first definition had to do with participation in sports, the second with musical instruments. Then there followed many, many articles on players and *seduction*. For me, reading all those articles was almost as bad as reading an erotic romance novel—I think. (Hand to God, I have never read one, but I can imagine!)

Obviously, from the way this guy looked at other women, he was an admirer of the opposite sex. But I didn't know if that qualified him as a player. And a mere kiss in broad daylight in a mall parking lot does not equate to a loving interest. But maybe after looking at other women, he was so thrilled to be with *me*, he'd wanted to show his affection. Or not.

I wished I could read his mind. I wished I wasn't so naive and inexperienced. What would be the proper etiquette in a situation like this?

Etiquette! That was it! I was going to write a thank-you note. I could then insert a little bit of humor (after all, that was in my profile!) and maybe find out, without making a fool of myself, whether or not this kiss was meaningless to him.

I fired off a quick email thanking him for the lunch. In case the poor guy had any inkling that I over-conversationalized a bit, I proved him right by going on and thanking him for the kiss. But why stop there? I added that he was very nice, but since I felt "sisterly" toward him (that was the humor part), did the kiss make us incestuous? LOL! I sent it.

I figured I wouldn't hear back from him, that this would end my sweeter-than-wine-kiss obsession, and it would evaporate from my memory.

I got a return email from him. No, evidently he took my email as a challenge. He definitely didn't have incestuous feelings toward *me*, he wrote, so *next time*, he'd have to put *more* into it.

Wait. What?! Oh, no! I couldn't believe what I'd done. What exactly did he mean, *next* time? *More* into it? Hmm. More. Into the kiss. Lord, help me. I should *not* have read all those sexually explicit details on Google. If a kiss made me fantasize, what exactly was going to be in store for me in the future if I were to receive a romantic kiss? He was probably just saying that. It was just flirtation, right? He was a player, for heaven's sake, and I didn't need to "play" back! I needed to calm down. I'd probably never hear from him again. I would *not* answer him. Case closed. Then my mind began to wander. But what if . . .

Just how do older single women prepare for kissing? I thought. *My lips are old. What do they feel like to the kisser? Are they too rough? They've thinned through the years—can a man even find them on my face, really? Or should I make them bigger, using lipstick? That wouldn't work. I'd probably just end up looking like a clown. Would a lip injection be the ticket? Ouch. Forget trying to make them look bigger. But I could work on making them softer.*

I scoured my bathroom closet to see if there was anything in there I could use for soft, kissable lips. I know one is supposed to toss old makeup, but some of the stuff I'd bought years ago was expensive, and if it was good quality, it ought to last a long time, right? I hunted through towels, vaporizers, nebulizers, first aid medicine, toilet paper, and soap. Finally, in the back corner of the top shelf of my bathroom closet, I found the basket with my old cosmetics.

It had a layer of the white dust that comes from toilet paper rolls, so I wiped that off and started hunting for lip gloss . . . and then got sidetracked checking out all the "new" makeup I found that I'd forgotten. I had no idea I'd ever owned so much. What precisely determines if one is a hoarder? But it *was* kind of like Christmas to pull out the various beauty products and check them out in the bathroom mirror.

There was a bunch of mascara. Good! I wouldn't have to buy any for a while, which, since I was single, would be a good way to save money.

I couldn't even pull the brush out of the first tube, so that went in the garbage can. The other practically brand-new tube was silver mascara. When would I have bought *silver* mascara? I didn't even remember when that was popular. I almost set it aside for Halloween. But at this age, would I really need anything to make me look more silvered than I already was? At Halloween, if I want to scare anyone, I just wouldn't wear *any* makeup! I tossed that tube, too. On second glance, all the other tubes looked old, so they got tossed also. So much for saving money.

Ooh, eye shadow! I knew electric blue might make my green eyes pop, but when I opened the lid to it, the blue had faded to an almost ice-colored death-look. *Do not want to look older than I am*, I thought. *Toss.*

Concealer. I opened it, and it was an ugly yellow

concealer. I tried to remember what I'd once read about which concealers are used to hide blemishes. There are yellow and green concealers. Was this yellow stuff antique medication left over from my teen blemish years? Or was it newer, to hide age spots? I thought I might as well try it, so I dabbed a bit on some sun-damaged skin and peered into the mirror.

It looked like a big bruise had formed. A paper bag would've been better. *Throw it away!*

Makeup—ivory. *It looks kind of tan. And I'm not. Toss.*

Oh, good! Lipstick—ah—getting closer. I opened the tube and discovered there was only a nubbin left. A few years ago, I was trying to be economical and thought I could use a cotton swab to get the last vestige of color out and onto my lips. I felt much richer now, especially since this stuff was kind of purplish, so into the trash it went.

Finally! My search was rewarded. Lip gloss! I was relieved to see it appeared to still be in good shape. I carefully squeezed the tube and traced around my lips, then filled it in. It was kind of like what I used to do when I used puffy paints back in the 1980s to do crafts with my kids. I peered at my image a bit more closely, smacked my lips together, and was thrilled that I now had lips that glistened with youthful dewiness. *Yes!*

I couldn't help but smile at my reflection. Not bad. This was what my dates would see, and they'd be sure to be attracted to these luscious-looking lips. I got a little closer to the mirror. If I pretended I was the guy, and my reflection in the mirror was me, what would he see this close up?

He'd be sure to notice the twinkle in my eyes, and my pert little nose. Wait—was that a nose hair? Oh, rats! Well, that threw me back to reality. How disgusting! It would be so much easier to just quit this dating stuff and not have to worry about my looks.

I debated for a minute about the foibles of being vain and the freedom I'd have to just be myself. But habits are hard to break, and I'd been fighting aging, I supposed, since I was twelve. That seems very young, I know, to have been worried about my looks. But I was, and I was too old to change now! All the experimenting my friends and I did with makeup when I was young stayed with me the rest of my life. When a dentist bonded the space between my front teeth when I was in my forties, I thanked God I'd been born in the twentieth century.

Back to my pretend close encounter of the male kind. I stared at my reflection. *Now what do I do?* I thought. *Who's going to tell me how to kiss? What if I'm so inured to all the platonic kissing that I subconsciously send a message that I really am more sisterly than siren in my oral friendliness? Eeek. What to do?*

The more I stared at the mirror, the more I felt this dating thing was getting a bit scary . . . and yet exciting. But scarier than dating, to me, was the possibility of making a fool of myself. I was sure some of these guys I might meet had been married more than once. Probably most of them had dated more than I had, counting the teen years. Including my high-school sweetheart, I'd kissed three *boys*. That meant, not counting my platonic "boyfriends,"

I'd never been kissed by another *man* . . . until the parking lot goodbye.

Time warp back to my teens. In my family, all six of us kids shared one bathroom. Evidently, some of the kids would take advantage of finally being alone in there and would practice kissing. I remember my mom disgustedly wiping lip prints off the bathroom mirror and asking which one of us kids messed it up. She had to have known either my brother or I had done it, because we were the only ones tall enough to reach it. I'm almost positive it was my brother. But then again, at that age, he didn't like girls. Oh, well. I sure wasn't going to go around now, kissing mirrors at my age!

Or . . . well, maybe practicing in the mirror might not be a bad idea. Who was going to see? Besides my dog Ralphie, and he wouldn't care.

If I did practice kissing, whom should I pretend to kiss? I'd always had a crush on David Cassidy, but I wondered how tall he was. Well, I knew I had to crane my neck up to look at my latest date, so . . . I closed my eyes and leaned in for what I was sure would be a dreamy and very long kiss.

If I'd thought it would be romantic to use a bathroom mirror to pretend to lip-lock with someone, I'd used the wrong adjective. It was *not* romantic. Pathetic was more like it.

I tried to separate my lips from his. Or rather, from the mirror. Just like the puffy paints I used to use, the old lip gloss had fast turned into a gooey, sticky mess. For one terrifying second, I stared cross-eyed at my mirror image, and my lips stretched like some sort of Silly Putty as I pulled away.

When they did pop off, they left what looked to be a glob of petroleum jelly petrifying before my eyes. My penance for all the lip-marks my mom had had to wipe off was a good ten minutes of Windex, ammonia, and a razor blade to remove the traces of my reversion to juvenile pucker-practice.

I tossed the lip gloss away. Never again would I practice kissing myself in a mirror. The tiles in the shower and my bedroom pillow, maybe. But never, ever again would I mess with the mirror!

New Hobby

Webster's Dictionary defines "hobby" as an activity or interest pursued for pleasure or relaxation and not as a main occupation. Hobbies require dedication and commitment, and should be enjoyable. They can be a diversion from real life, they can be something totally new and different, or they can be an interest you've always had, but now can pursue in a leisurely fashion.

After just a few weeks of cyber-dating, I was hooked. For the rest of the summer, it was my new hobby. I'd wake up mornings and immediately open my email. I checked my email before I left for work. I checked again at break time, lunch, afternoon break time, after work, at supper, and at least three or four more times before I shut down my computer and went to bed.

I began to wonder if I should retire from work so this could be my main occupation. But then it wouldn't be a hobby, would it? My initial hesitation in dating by using the Internet had fast disappeared, as my ego continued to be built up every day that I checked my email. I felt like I had the first time I visited a candy store and had to pick out only one piece. There were too many choices. If I was lucky enough to get a *formerly* annoying electronic "wink" from someone, I felt like a diva!

For a girl who'd had old-fashioned standards as a teen, I quickly ditched the one about waiting for the male to make the first move. I became totally at ease firing off the first email to a potential date. This may have been my new hobby, but the competitive side in me took over, and thanks to my "Roving Reporter" email crush, I learned to strike first before any other women could nab "the good ones."

Speaking of competition, I began to wonder what other women in my general vicinity were on the hunt. I knew a few single older women in my town, and I began to suspect they might be on the same mission I was. I also knew what happened when a neighbor and a very wealthy businessman had lost their wives. Within a mere six months of becoming single, they both became ensnared by man-hungry younger women. Honestly, some women have no compunction. Girls, give us older ladies a chance!

I could at least find out more about what was in other women's profiles that enticed gentlemen. I was still a bit unsure whether I'd written the best profile possible in order to find a decent date. Since there were no manuals for us "singlets," what were other ladies putting on their profiles?

It didn't take a lot of detective work to find out. I simply pulled up my profile and changed it from "Woman Seeking Man" to "Man Seeking Woman." Just for a few minutes.

Bingo! There they were—and there was an acquaintance

of mine who had moved out of state! I quickly read the autobiographies of my rivals, studied their photos, and decided we were all different enough that there was no competition among us.

But my friend—how could she still be single? She was cute as a bug, young-looking, and her write-up was impressive. I hit "Like" so that she would know how impressed I was with her profile and made a mental note to get her phone number and give her a call. It would be fun to share stories about dating—*and* she was now miles away, so she wouldn't be looking at any guys in my territory who wouldn't move, even for love!

I didn't realize at the time that she could open her "like" from this new "man" and see *my* profile. When I learned about this months later, I could only hope she knew me better than to think I was either spying on her or interested in her as a date! Geesh!

Then came a lull . . . probably because it was summer, holiday time, and people were extra busy or gone on vacation. There were no new matches for several days. This meant I could take a really hard look at the guys I'd quickly passed over for one reason or another. Some of them were horrible spellers, just too desperate-sounding, or had profiles with lots of red flags. Was I really so hobby-driven that I would look at a guy who had been divorced four times and hated kids? Well, I looked, so I guess that answer was yes. Time to give my hobby a rest.

Too Good to be True

The summer slump was over, and I was riding high on all the matches that were coming my way. By now, I could easily pick and choose which ones I was really interested in. I replied to everyone who "winked," "liked," or "favorited" me, thanking them, telling them whether I was interested in pursuing a further connection. It was almost like working a conveyor belt.

As the matches appeared before me, I could select or skip them. I began to take for granted that I would probably be meeting people electronically the rest of my life. Some of these I would email for a while, some I would meet in person, and some I would never have contact with.

One day a match appeared who really stood out. I suddenly had thoughts that maybe one day I'd be on a commercial, touting that this electronic dating was really real and worked. The profile looked too good to be true. He was good-looking, with a smile that I expected would shoot twinkles from his teeth. He liked everything I did, including my very favorite TV show. That was a biggie--an unexpected biggie!

Of all the matches I'd looked at, and they were now numbering in the hundreds, he was the only one who loved USA's show *Psych*. It was a witty, sharp, and humorous show. I'd never seen an episode that hadn't made me laugh, and I could barely wait each week for a new episode. I owned all the seasons of it on DVD, and when it was on hiatus, I survived by replaying each season just to get my "*Psych* fix."

Here, right in front of me, was a match surely made in television heaven. I couldn't wait to contact "SIKELUVR." (Okay, so he couldn't spell *Psych*, but at that point I didn't care.) I hoped he would respond, and sure enough, the very next day he did.

I was thrilled. Would he like to meet sometime? Yes, he would. Hooray. This *was* too good to be true. However, his next email said he was headed down to a relative's home in Arizona. From there, he might mosey on over to either New Mexico, or the Appalachians, or both, so he'd get back in touch with me.

I'd never before known anyone who could just, all of a sudden, "mosey" to two totally different places on the map. In my *Psych*-enamored condition, I was in awe. What a man he must be—willing to go where the wandering stars led him. *And* he loved *Psych*.

I promised him I would record the next few weeks of *Psych* episodes for him, and maybe that could be our first date—to watch those episodes when he returned? He was *so* thankful! "What a great idea! You would really do that for me?" he wrote.

"Just have a safe trip, and hurry back!" I eagerly responded. "I can even fix popcorn!"

I was almost smug about the way I had handled securing a date. I bet he'd never known a woman who was willing to DVR and pop popcorn for him. I could hardly wait for him to return to Iowa. It was almost like *Psych* hiatus time, only I didn't have any DVDs of this guy. I was giddy with anticipation. I hardly looked at any other matches, because I knew in my heart that this guy just had to be made for me.

One week, then two weeks, went by. No correspondence from him at all. By the end of the third week, I began re-reading "Sike's" last emails to me to see if I had missed anything, but no. Nothing popped out at me. I was missing my new friend, and I hadn't even met Sike in person yet. Finally, I pulled up his profile so I could gaze at his wonderful smile again, and imagine how his teeth would shine as he smiled at me in the light of the TV as we watched *Psych* together.

His profile was *blocked*! What does that mean? What would Gus or Shawn of *Psych* fame do? I checked all the dating site's definitions of the various words they used. Here it was. "Blocking" a profile was the equivalent of slamming a door shut and locking it. *Oh, no,* I thought. *That can't be right. Maybe he blocked his profile so that other women wouldn't be bugging him, since he probably feels the same way about me that I do about him. Yeah. That has to be it.*

Or . . . horrible thought! Had Sike *died* on his trip? Or had he met some female on the road, and they'd decided to cross the country by motorcycle, like a Harley-Davidson Lancelot and his Guinevere? *I* hate *motorcycles,* I decided.

Had my perfect match taken the chicken way out of dumping me—before I could even technically be dumped? The fog of enamored fantasy lifted, and I came to my senses. Well, it didn't take a *Psych*-ic to figure this out. This guy was a jerk who'd messed with me! I blocked him, too. At least it was a lesson learned.

From English Lit class forty-six years ago, I recalled a quote:

"For of all sad words of tongue or pen, the saddest are these: 'It might have been.'"
    — John Greenleaf Whittier

"NEXT!"
    — Becky Beaman

Cheap Dates

It wasn't unusual, of course, at my age, to have a lot of potential dates that were semi- or fully retired. I was captivated by their profiles, which heralded their time to *travel* to exotic places; *dine* at fabulous new restaurants; *explore* new interests; and simply *enjoy* life's leisure activities like golf, plays, and resorts. I was still working, and found myself a bit envious that these people had the time and money to do all that. But if they included me in on a date, I was willing to help them travel, dine, explore, and enjoy! I had a lot to learn, it turned out.

Take, for example, my date with a match I'll call "Ebenezer Scrooge." I was still unsure of old-age dating protocol at this point. He had invited me to meet for coffee at a downtown café. We sat outside for a while talking, and it was pleasant, but nothing exciting.

When our visit was done and we were getting ready to leave, I realized that he was not making any attempt to extract his wallet. Surely he wasn't going to stiff the café for a couple of drinks? I thought of a recent letter I'd read in "Dear Abby" about sharing expenses on a date. *Should I offer to pay?* I thought. *I don't want him to think I'm chintzy!*

"Would you like me to get this?" I asked.

Ebenezer actually hesitated, shrugged, and then mumbled something about paying. Oh, dear! I hoped I hadn't embarrassed him. Maybe he was really poor. I should have glanced again at his profile before the date to see what category his income was. To save face for him, I quickly went to the counter and paid the two whole dollars.

I'm ashamed to admit that I was wrestling with feelings of sympathy versus annoyance that he hadn't jumped right up and paid. What the heck did this guy think a date *was*, anyway? After all, it had been his idea to meet here. He should have ordered water if he was that cheap . . . or maybe his Social Security check was late. I thought I'd better give him the benefit of the doubt.

So it pleasantly surprised me when, in a few minutes, he looked at his watch, pointed at a nearby restaurant, and asked me if I'd like a sandwich—his treat! I tried flashing my most brilliant and sweetest smile, in humility. He was probably just as new to this whole dating thing as I was. Or maybe one of his kids had told him dating nowadays meant going Dutch treat, and he'd chosen to pay for the more expensive part of the date. How sweet!

We both must have gotten over the initial first-time meeting jitters, because we actually ended up spending two more hours together talking, laughing, and really enjoying Baby Boomer conversation. "Baby Boomer conversation" is finding out what cartoons we used to watch on Saturday mornings, recalling that Micky Dolenz of the Monkees was *Circus Boy* Corky when he was little, and remembering the name of Sky King's plane (Songbird). As a matter of fact, I was enjoying this date so much that time was flying by! I decided that maybe Ebenezer might be worth checking out on another date.

Evidently he had the same feeling, because he asked me if I'd like to meet again. Woo-hoo, a second date! We gave each other a little hug, and I headed over to my car, which was parked near his.

However, I did notice that he didn't leave a tip, even though we'd eaten our sandwiches in the first fifteen minutes and then sat there taking up a booth for hours. Hmm. But I chose to be positive and nice! Maybe he'd slipped a tip to the waitress when I hadn't been looking. Yeah. That had to be it.

The next weekend was our second date, and this time we met at a casino. Ebenezer showed up, and we started our conversation from where we left off the week before. I felt like I really knew this guy. We sat in a vacant eating area on a floor of the casino, so we could talk and laugh like a couple of young kids in a secret clubhouse. This was great! "Would you like something to drink?" he finally asked.

"Sure." I started to pick up one of the menus from the middle of the table.

"Oh, no need to bother with that," he told me. This casino, renowned for its delicious food, also provided *free* coffee and pop, available to all the gamblers!

I sat there watching him, debating whether or not I

should point out that we hadn't gambled yet, so maybe we didn't qualify for the freebies. But I had to give him the benefit of the doubt. Maybe his plan for the date was that we would go gambling pretty soon. After all, I was sure the casino could afford free pop and coffee. Heck, yes!

After lots more talking and several large cups of pop and coffee, we needed to take a break to check out the restrooms. The first thing I did was freshen up my makeup, brush my hair, and make a quick smile in the mirror so I could see if my teeth looked yellow or pop-colored!

I beat Ebenezer back out and ended up standing in the hallway, looking at pictures and paintings of various casinos, gambling machines, and horses. After quite awhile, I began to wonder if maybe he'd come out first and had gone looking for me. Or had he just left? Paul Simon's song "50 Ways to Leave Your Lover" suddenly popped into my paranoid mind. Just as I began to work my insecurities into high gear, Ebenezer walked out of the men's room.

"Oh, there you are," he said, with a big grin on his face. I felt a warm glow spread over me and melt away my self-doubt. He was really happy to see me! He grabbed one of my hands, and we headed toward the gaming area.

"Well, that was profitable!" he announced, and his grin got even bigger.

Huh? I tried to think if I'd ever heard that sentence uttered after emerging from a restroom. It seemed out of place, but my curiosity got the better of me. I thought I might regret this, but I couldn't refrain: "Profitable?"

If his grin had gotten any wider, his cheeks would've been touching his ears. He opened the fist of his other hand and revealed a bunch of coins. "There's probably four or five dollars here," he said proudly.

My jaw dropped. "Awesome! I didn't know they have slot machines in there. They don't in the ladies' room!" I was impressed with my date's gambling ability.

He squeezed my hand, lovingly, I thought. Then he shook his head. "Nah. I found these!"

"Wow!" Again, a profound utterance from me. "Just lying on the counter?"

"No."

"On the floor?"

"No."

This was fun. He was actually teasing me! "I give up. Where, then?" I asked, squeezing his other hand in excitement.

"In the toilet."

In the toilet? I stopped dead, and pulled my hand from his. I began to wipe it on my jeans, and my eyes darted around the casino to see where I could find some industrial-strength soap to wash it.

Ebenezer stopped and finally noticed my look of horror. "Oh, don't worry," he assured me. "I washed them in the sink."

"Oh, my God." I know the look that I gave him was one of total disgust. "I'd have *paid* you five dollars to not have picked those up."

He didn't even seem to be slightly embarrassed or

ashamed. He seemed as enthralled with his find as if he'd panned for gold and hit the mother lode.

"Well, I didn't want to let all that money go to waste," he said earnestly.

His unintended pun about "waste" made my stomach curdle. I could only groan. By this time, we'd entered the slots area, and Ebenezer quickly plopped down to deposit his treasure from the toilet into the machine. I hoped whoever emptied the slot machines wore gloves.

I stood there for almost thirty seconds. *Okay,* I thought. *I'm on this dating site, not only to find male companionship, but possibly . . . very remotely, but possibly all the same . . . to find a potential husband.* I stared at this man, now a total stranger, and a scenario flashed through my mind of being the future Mrs. Ebenezer Scrooge: scrounging around public toilets, picking up pop cans to redeem them for deposit money, or even having to sell my blood in order to survive.

I muttered something about remembering I had to babysit my grandkids, and practically ran out of the casino before he could ask me out again.

I guess I'd had Ebenezer pegged correctly from the beginning. I just wished I had listened to myself!

I thought of a plan for the future: *One, I need to find out if the retiree dates are on limited incomes, no matter what their profiles say. And two, don't waste time on the cheap-os. It could turn into a hazmat case.*

Bernie—Or Dead Man Talking

This particular man was one I had overlooked a few times before, purely on account of his profile picture. To me, he was a dead ringer for Bernie—the character from *Weekend at Bernie's*, the dark comedy movie from the 1980s in which the title character got bumped off by the mob at the beginning of the picture. He was in about every scene in the movie, though, so that his two bumbling employees could pretend he was still alive in order to enjoy a weekend vacation at Bernie's beach mansion.

In real life, this Bernie was very much alive. After getting over his likeness to a dead guy, I studied what he'd written. His profile was awesome! He loved to travel to Florida. Any place with a beach was fabulous. As a matter of fact, he was definitely a traveler who loved the outdoors. Nothing like sailing a boat and having the breeze blowing through his hair, he wrote. He sent me a nice little email the first time and said he thought we would make a good match, and he seemed very nice. I had to admit, he really did sound like a fun guy to be around.

Best of all, his profile had a second picture showing him leaning up against . . . wait for it . . . *a Corvette Stingray convertible!* When I was sixteen, I worshipped Corvettes. I coveted Corvettes. I lusted after those beautiful, sporty, sexy little Corvettes.

I *had* to have a date with this guy. Maybe we could go to a drive-in. I bought a can of heavy-duty hairspray in anticipation of a breezy, beautiful ride.

I should have bought a can of mace.

The date started out okay. Bernie wanted to meet at a sports bar about twenty minutes from me. Then we could go for a walk somewhere if we wanted to. I was a bit disappointed to hear that, because I'd dreamed about riding in that Corvette, but maybe he'd at least let me sit inside his car for a minute so that I could take a selfie!

I only had a minute's lead on him as I sat inside the restaurant. On hearing the rev of a motor, I looked out the window in the reception area and noticed his little sports car as he drove up. I stepped outside to meet him.

He left his sunglasses on as we entered the restaurant (very Bernie-like), and asked me if I'd mind sitting outside because it was sunny and breezy, and he *loved* fresh air. (*Straight from his profile—he must say that a lot,* I thought.)

I agreed to sit outside, even though I would have described the weather as boiling hot and gusty. I found out very quickly that Bernie was much windier than anything Mother Nature had to throw at me!

He first started out comparing our childhood families for similarities. We had both grown up Catholic. We were both from large families. I got in a sentence or two about living on a farm when I was ten, and having my own Shetland pony.

That was the first and last sentence I spoke for about fifteen minutes, if you don't count all the "mmmms" and "uh-huhs" I was able to mutter now and then. I don't quite know how Bernie managed to get from siblings fighting to the fact that he'd lost a beloved relative years ago, but at that point I was allowed to murmur, "I'm so sorry."

He was the first date I had of the ones who had been divorced who seemed quite bitter about it. According to him, he had been married (for many years) to the most heinous female in creation. If I ever wanted to meet the devil, Bernie ranted at me, he'd introduce me to his ex!

I found myself wondering if it was a sin to side with Satan this once.

He finally started pontificating on how judgmental people are (especially his ex), but that they shouldn't be. I started to say that perhaps he had misjudged his former wife, but of course, I never got the chance to blurt it out. He repeatedly mentioned that "people can't judge others; they can't even really know others." I don't know if he was trying to drill that into me so I would give him a chance at dating, but it was a lost cause for him. After only forty-five minutes of listening to him go on and on about judging, or not judging, people, I had not only judged him, but tried and convicted him, and would have loved to hang him high just to get him to shut up for a single minute!

His next oration was on his career as a hospital practitioner, from which he was recently retired. I was treated to graphic descriptions of people dying, and of how, since he was a people person, he'd also had to help the survivors by telling them it was okay to cry. I was starting to tear up myself, but it had nothing to do with sympathy for the departed or their survivors. I wondered if he had talked those poor souls to death.

Bernie moved on to the topic of what can happen to naive single women like me. He didn't notice my indignant stare at his sunglasses at that crack, because he was proudly warning me, again in graphic detail, about murders, near-death beatings, and rapes that he'd seen the results of during the time he worked in the hospital. He was certain these things occurred because women would break up after a date or two, and that electronic dating could sometimes be a horrible thing. "Yes! Most definitely," was all I was able to say, as I nodded my head vehemently in agreement.

"Or," I piped up, as he took a breath, "I'm sure there are *men* who get beaten up by their dates, probably because they don't—"

I was going to finish saying, *let the woman have a turn talking*, but Bernie came alive again and interrupted me to expound on *that* topic. I signaled a waiter and ordered a diet Mountain Dew, mainly so I would have something else to look at other than my bored reflection in Bernie's sunglasses. Still he chattered, about what, I could no longer comprehend.

It's amazing, I thought to myself as Bernie's voice droned on and on, *how ingrained politeness is in me. Why can't I muster up the gumption to just interrupt him forcefully and say this date is as dead as he looks, and I'm leaving?* I wondered if this would qualify somewhat as Stockholm syndrome, where the hostages related to their captors. Whatever was wrong with me, I was going to have to suffer awhile longer, it appeared!

When I couldn't get a word in edgewise, I decided to let him read my body language. I stared down at my drink and counted the ice cubes in it. I smiled at a baby at the next table and started waving and cooing at it. I crossed my arms in front of me, and I seriously considered faking narcolepsy and catching some shut-eye.

Bernie eventually did ask me a few questions, but whenever I answered, he would again interrupt and go off on a tangent, triggered by something that I had partially said. I was a little bit fascinated that he could talk so long without having to take a drink, or even run out of things to say. It seemed he felt he was an expert on everything. I empathized with his ex-wife, and wished I knew how she'd gotten away from this "talk-aholic."

I tried to do what Bernie had done, by interrupting, but it didn't work. There would just be two babbling voices, and people at the surrounding tables looked at us quizzically. I ran out of things to say first, and he always won—although he seemed oblivious to the fact that I'd even tried to speak.

He kept talking about how important it was to act young and take care of oneself. He hardly took a breath before he segued into telling me many people had guessed his age to be forty-nine (he was sixty-five), at which point I tried to stifle a laugh because I thought he was kidding. He looked like he was at least ten years older than I was! If my dad had let her, my mom could have pretended to be a real cougar and dated him! He evidently mistook my laughter for delight that he looked so young.

Bernie asked me if I thought he looked like the picture on his profile. I totally missed seizing the opportunity to truthfully tell him he looked a little more "mature" than his profile picture. I gathered that he was hoping I'd say yes, and then he would tell me it was a picture that was ten or twenty years old—taken when he was *much* younger!

I instead told him that he reminded me of a coworker who had the same mustache, goatee, and hair color. I didn't tell him the coworker was long retired, and had dyed his hair more years than I had been alive. Drat! Another missed opportunity.

This went on for four hours, with no food in sight, even though when Bernie stopped to take a breath, I said I needed to get home to feed the dog his *supper*. I tried to think of a nice way to leave. There wasn't one.

Finally I just stood up, which made him pause for a second. I said drily, "Well, this has certainly been a great way to kill an afternoon. Sorry, but I really must go!"

Bernie attempted to be gentlemanly by saying he would walk me to my car. Then he stayed seated and proceeded to talk awhile longer. I just stood there, fuming. I don't know why I didn't just turn and leave. I couldn't really believe this type of date had actually happened. I had to learn to be hard-nosed, it appeared, and I really do hate conflict. But I was beginning to hate this guy more—Corvette Stingray Convertible or not!

I started to leave by edging my way toward the patio gate. I said goodbye, and Bernie said he'd like to see me again.

No way! was what I almost said. Sixty years of being a polite good girl took over, though. I told him truthfully that I didn't feel we had a dating connection, and that I was going to take to heart his advice not to do electronic dating anymore, because I believed him when he said it could be dangerous.

At that, Bernie took his sunglasses off at last. He made a pouty face, which made his crepey and droopy old-man eyelids all the more prominent, and said, "Oh, that's only with the wrong guy. Not me!"

I just shrugged.

Then he said, "I'm really disappointed—I feel connected to you." Yeah, I felt *connected*, too . . . like electrodes in a state death chamber.

"Hug?" he asked. I hesitated because I couldn't believe he'd even ask that.

He took that as a yes, grabbed me, and held on, while I tried politely and gently to extract myself. Oh, what the hell! I was never going to see this guy again, so I got my feet to go backward, slipped down, and pushed my way out of his grasp.

"Bye!" I yelled.

I couldn't get to my car fast enough, and I locked the doors. I didn't even glance at him as I drove away, but out of the corner of my eye, I saw him posing next to his 'Vette—that car that I would never covet again! I could smell his cologne on my cheek. Yuck!

Once I was home, I took a shower, ravenously ate some leftovers from the fridge, and threw my DVD of *Weekend at Bernie's* in the trash. Then I posted the following on Facebook:

It's official, I have met my MATCH! Not, however, in a love connection, nor even as friends. I met a man this afternoon who out-talked me. I mean, he so out-talked me that I am humbled, and still in shock. How can someone not stop for breath for four hours?

Ready for My Close-Up, Mr. DeMille!

One of my matches enjoyed watching movies, something I had said I liked to do, too. And I truly do. I've gone alone to a movie theatre once or twice. It was more fun when I went with a group of my girlfriends, though. I imagined it would be a lot more fun going with a date!

We had originally set the meeting up as dinner and a movie—something that sounded really nice. We had planned to meet at the mall, go to one of the two non-fast-food restaurants there at 5:45 p.m., then catch the 7:05 showing of an action movie.

While I'm not a huge fan of action movies, I thought it would be interesting. I was eager to meet this man, and thought getting to talk to him ahead of the movie at dinner would be nice. It might have been, but I never got the chance.

I got a phone call at four p.m. the day of the date from this guy—I'll call him Cecil (as in DeMille, a famous Hollywood film producer from 1914 to 1956). It seemed some of his family had dropped in unexpectedly, they were all going to have supper together, and would I mind terribly if we pushed the movie back to the nine p.m. show? And, again with abject apologies, would I either like to have dinner *after* that time, or would I want to go ahead and eat on my own before the movie?

I had been planning on going on this date for several days, so I had not planned on having anything to eat at home that night. The *late* show? This man was my age—what time was *his* bedtime? I could stay up until the ten o'clock news was over, but barely. And another thing—I'd had to cut short my visit with my kids to come home before four to get ready and allow enough time to drive to the mall so I would make the 5:45 dinner.

"Oh, of course," I said cheerily. "I'll just eat on my own, and the later show will be fine." I hadn't screwed up enough courage, or thought on my feet fast enough, to ask him a few questions. Why hadn't I just asked him to reschedule the date? For that matter, why hadn't *he* just suggested we reschedule? Why hadn't he told his family he had plans? Poor guy. We hadn't even met, and already I had assigned him minus three points. But maybe actually meeting him in person would boost his ratings.

One peanut butter and jelly sandwich and over four hours later, I was seated in the mall near the theatres. It was crowded there, as any Friday night at the movies normally is. I waited . . . and waited . . . and waited. I checked my phone—no calls from Cecil. I made plans to head home and go to bed if he didn't show up by nine.

I had just stood up and started toward the exit door when Cecil rushed in. We recognized each other from our profile pictures. He seemed genuinely distraught about keeping me waiting, and also very happy to meet me. We shook hands, and then he started to tell me what had happened and why he was so late. His mother was elderly, he explained, and didn't get out often, so when his sister and her husband and kids stopped by with his mom, he . . . "Well, we can talk after the show," he said abruptly, after glancing toward the lines to the ticket sales counter.

He grabbed my elbow, steered me to a line, and purchased the two tickets. It was ten after nine by then, but he stopped at the popcorn counter and asked if I'd like something to eat. By that time, the peanut butter and jelly was a mere memory, and my stomach was growling at the smell of butter and salt. I said yes, and he ordered one extra-large tub of popcorn, obviously for the both of us. I carried the two cups of soft drinks he'd also bought.

We found our theatre, entered, and walked down the long corridor. I was looking ahead at the movie screen, and turned to Cecil to ask if Tom Cruise was in any other upcoming movies, because the trailer that was playing sure looked like the ones I'd seen for this movie.

Before he could answer me, the crowd let out a collective gasp as our hero Tom did something awesome that I missed. I had just turned to find a seat—and I gasped, too. It looked like the theatre was full.

"Where are we going to sit? It's full!" I whispered.

Cecil looked a little dismayed, too, but then said, "They wouldn't have sold us tickets if it was totally full."

Well, obviously there were two seats left because we were the last ones in. But the problem was not only that we were late enough that the movie had started, but the two seats were *not together*.

Cecil pointed toward the front of the theatre, where one empty seat sat at the far end of the second row. "You go ahead and take that one. I'll try to find another," he said gallantly. Then he reached for his soft drink. "I'll meet you in the lobby when it's over."

He turned away and disappeared into the darkness. With my half of the popcorn, I might add.

If I was a teenager again, I could have made it to my seat somewhat more gracefully than the sixty-one-year-old me did that night. Trying to walk down a row of movie theatre seats is not a feat accomplished gracefully, even when the row is not filled with people who have purchased drinks and food. I have night blindness, which means I can't easily see in the dark when some idiot in the row is slouched in his seat with his long legs fully extended out into my path. I was trying to duck down to avoid having the shadow of my head play on the giant screen, and sidestepping along the row. I was praying that my "best" side wasn't knocking over others' drinks or popcorn, when all of a sudden, I tripped on the feet of the lounging gentleman. ("Gentleman" is not the term I muttered at the time.) In my hunched-over state, I went lurching rapidly toward the end of the row like a sidling, but lumbering, crab. I even spilled a little bit of pop, unfortunately *not* on the slouched culprit. I kept apologizing and excusing myself to the other patrons as I stumbled over to my seat.

When the date (me) is seated in the front of the theatre, getting cricks in her neck, and wishing she had some delicious popcorn to eat, and the dater (Cecil) has found a seat in the nosebleed section where all the young couples go to kiss, text, and do other assorted unmentionable things, all I can say is: "This date was dead to begin with."

The good part was that I ended up really enjoying the movie, except after it was over, I had trouble hearing. I think my eardrums ruptured at the high-decibel volume. It took me a few minutes to adjust my eyesight when the movie was over and the lights came up, but yes, it was a decent movie. Eventually, I made it to the lobby with the rest of the herd of moviegoers.

The bad part was when I finally spied my date. The first thing I noticed was that there was no popcorn! I just hoped my stomach wouldn't growl if we went somewhere. But evidently Cecil was as tired as I was, because after some lame conversation, punctuated with a lot of "huhs" and "whats" because we were both temporarily theatre-deaf, we realized that other than the movie, we really didn't have much in common to talk about.

I thanked him, told him that I needed to get home to go to bed, and that there didn't seem to be any sparks. Maybe if we were young again, this would have been the start of the evening, but at eleven p.m., it was the middle of the night for me! Besides, my ears were still ringing, and

I didn't think I'd even be able to hear him if we did have any sort of conversation.

I made it home by half past eleven, ate one more peanut butter and jelly sandwich, put some analgesic heat rub on my neck, and hit the sack. I decided if I ever went to another movie, it would be in comfy clothes and no makeup, with a full stomach, and no date!

One Hot Date!

If it's possible for seniors to ever describe a date as a "hot" one—and I don't mean because of menopausal hot flashes—I can actually say I had a bona fide hot date! It was almost sacrilegious because it was on a Sunday, and we definitely got steamy. The date was filled with heavy breathing, panting, and two bodies gleaming with sweat in a very secluded area. I even slapped him once.

One profile picture of a match intrigued me. It was a professionally done photograph of a distinguished-looking man in a dress shirt, tie, and suit. His hair was slicked back, revealing a slightly receding hairline, and he was graying a bit at the temples. He looked like he must be rather prominent, and I guessed him to be in his late sixties and probably at least six feet tall, or even taller.

Since that mode of dress and the quality of the picture were an anomaly in the profiles I had to choose from, I had to take a second glance. He had an interesting face, and had five other pictures on his page that he'd labeled. He explained that the main photo had been a media shot for a case he'd covered.

Ooh! This guy must have an interesting job! I thought.

I checked out his other pictures. I double-checked the first photo, and then looked at the others again. There was such a difference in dress and demeanor that at first I thought it had to be an entirely different person. The second picture was of a man in a T-shirt and hiking shorts, with a mustache, a goatee, and a boyish grin on his face, slouched against a boulder. His hair was a little disheveled and fell forward on his face, making him look young and roguish. That appealed to me—a whole different look to this guy! A chameleon! He had other pictures, but I kept returning to the hiking one because he looked so happy and almost impish.

I began to read his profile. *Hmm . . . an attorney. Has two homes, one here and one out West. Mmm-hmmm! Even more interesting.* His divorce had hit him out of the blue—his wife had evidently found someone more interesting, and he'd had no idea. He wrote he wasn't interested in serial dating, being friends with benefits, or finding a gal pal, but wanted a serious, life-long relationship. I decided to take a chance and satisfy my curiosity about him.

I fired off what had become my standard email, a *very* shortened version of my earlier ones (my "Roving Reporter" would have been proud). According to all of my friends who had helped me draft it, my email was sweet, intelligent, and designed to make sure whoever read it would be dying to meet me.

I waited a day, then two. No response. I waited one more day to make sure he wasn't on a tough legal case, and then decided to move on. But the fourth day, I got an email from him!

My heart quickened. I hoped he sounded like the happy guy I saw in the hiking picture. If I started corresponding with this man, I wondered if I'd better brush up on the legal terminology I'd learned in college forty years ago. I thought hard, searching for some terminology I could remember, but "shyster" was the only one that came to mind, so I gave that up.

Finally I opened his email and had to scan the page twice before I saw his answer. It was four words long. Four very puzzling words:

"CHECK WITH ME LATER."

Huh? I re-read it. Ooo-kay! This was really puzzling . . . and a little annoying. It was like he was issuing me an order. Just how much later? Later this afternoon? In a week? Who writes an answer like that? Could he have taken another second and added a "please" to the front of that command?

I decided to wait for a while. Maybe he'd write me again with an explanation. Maybe he was in the middle of some important legal meeting and stole a moment to quickly fire that message off to me! Yes, that was probably the reason! At least, for my ego's sake, that was the rationalization I was going to use.

Later, I checked my emails, but had nothing from him. By the next day, I was ready to toss this one in my "no-way" pile.

However, I kept thinking back to the smile and tousled hair in the hiking photo. Maybe he was out in the mountains somewhere and had had only enough bars on his cell to text me that message. So I decided to wait and check back.

It wasn't until a few days later that I remembered, and thought I'd try one last time. I fired off an email to him that read:

"IS THIS LATE ENOUGH?"

How concise a message was that? I was kind of proud of myself. Tit for tat, right? What's good for the goose is good for the gander. Quid pro quo. (I'd finally remembered some legal terminology, even though I wasn't quite sure what it meant. But it sounded good.) At least I'd have the final word, and in case I didn't ever hear back from him, maybe this guy would learn to write to prospective matches in a nicer fashion.

Actually, it was probably too bad that I wasn't going to meet him. His interests were exactly the same as mine, he was committed to staying fit, he liked every kind of animal known to humanity, and his favorite hot spots to dine, visit, or vacation were places with which I was very familiar.

One of those places stood out—it wasn't actually too far from where I lived: a simple little county park, known for its meandering trails, cool woods, and some Native American mounds. Duh! There it was! Why hadn't I caught that before?

I decided to try one last message. But it took me over an

hour to come up with one that I hoped would elicit some sort of response. It read:

"Counselor. Checking back. Hiking this Sunday, Indian Mounds Park, one p.m. Interested?"

When there was no answer the rest of the day, nor the day after, I gave up.

Saturday came and I was having coffee with some high-school friends. They were always eager to hear the latest about my, uh, "social" life, so I told them about the man (I called him "Perry" after *Perry Mason*, my favorite attorney show from the early 1960s) who had passed *a* bar exam, but not *mine*. I described him as a jerk for signing up on a dating site, but not corresponding, and they all agreed with me. I felt vindicated.

Then, in the middle of our conversation, my phone buzzed with a text. It was Perry! All it said was: "Sounds good. Call me, please," and a phone number. Unbelievable!

Of course, I got a high five from all my friends . . . except for the guys in the group. One of them even growled that *no way* would he let a daughter or sister of his meet someone in such a deserted place without knowing the guy first, especially since they'd all decided Perry was a jerk.

I assured everyone I'd checked my date's credentials (which had intrigued me even more), and that I was perfectly safe. After awhile, I figured that since I only had a little more than twenty-four hours to get ready, I'd better say goodbye, and I took off.

The warning words from my friends had actually been good ones, and I began to regret my decision to meet somewhere that truly was a bit isolated. I was prepared to ask to change the venue. (That phrase sounded so legal!)

I called Perry as soon as I got home. At least, I think it was him. All the preconceived notions I had about the man in the business suit with the curt email to me disappeared when I talked to the chatty and delightful voice that must have belonged to the guy in the hiking shorts. He loved my response to his first email, he said, and apologized for how short and cryptic it was, but he'd been busy and was only able to fire off a quick note. So I'd been right! He loved being back in Iowa, and was planning to stay here, he told me. Right now he was rooming with a friend, and trying to find time to visit places he used to go in Iowa before he'd moved out West. He hadn't been to that park for years, he gushed, and did it still have the three mounds? Yes, I told him.

He started asking me directions on how to get there, since it had been awhile. Unfortunately, I'm one of those people who talks with her hands. I can't keep track of how many times I've totally confused someone on the phone by saying things like "go over here, and then turn this way . . . "

I did this to poor Perry. I was in the middle of pointing and curving my arm to "show" him which road to take, when he interrupted and asked if I would like to meet first at a restaurant in town. Then he could either follow me out to the park, or if I wanted to, I could ride along with him.

I liked that he was a take-charge kind of guy, but in a nice way.

He went on to say he'd like to see if we had any chemistry. I was a little anxious at that. Maybe this was a guy's version of *my* version of "romantic sparks." Well, there would be only one way to find out. We made plans to meet at a restaurant in my town. The date was set, and if I'd had any second thoughts about meeting in an isolated place after my friends' warnings, they disappeared.

I spent the rest of the afternoon and following morning trying to find something that looked like hiking shorts that I could fit into, and ended up rushing to a local store to see if there existed a cute shirt in my size that would wick away perspiration. It was July, after all. Hot and humid July.

So it was that on a Sunday morning, I was planning to meet Perry at one p.m. Iowa weather kept its promise to be a hot and humid day. I decided to quickly mow my yard during the morning's cooler weather, since I had plenty of time. That way I would be able to get that weekend chore done, just in case the date went well and we ended up going out to dinner somewhere.

Mowing took longer than I'd thought, so I had to skip lunch and ended up rushing to shower. Then I had to decide whether to wear a pretty cotton tunic, or the polo shirt that wicked away moisture. I went for the polo shirt, not for its capability to keep me cooler, but because its color went well with what was going to pass as my hiking shorts.

I got to the restaurant on time. Right as I walked in, my cell rang. It was Perry, who apologized and said he'd be about fifteen minutes late.

"No problem," I assured him. That would give me time to order a drink, because I hadn't had time for lunch, and maybe he would decide to grab a bite to eat before we hiked.

I was sipping a diet pop and talking to my sister on my cell when he came in. Wow! He looked good—and younger than his pictures! That was a change from some of the other dates, for sure. I told Sis goodbye, flipped my phone closed, and shook hands with him.

He was definitely shorter than his professional shot had made him appear, but he looked athletic and had that youthful grin on his face that I had found so captivating in his other photo. The waitress appeared to ask if he'd like a drink, and checked to see if either of us would like anything to eat.

I was the one who'd finagled this date, and I'd suggested the time just so we wouldn't have to eat. That was because I was paranoid that I would get something stuck in my teeth and make a horrible impression. But I was absolutely starving by now. I hoped Perry would suggest we sit in the air-conditioned restaurant and at least order some fries or nachos, or something. But he didn't ask me if I wanted anything else. He just got water for himself.

We visited for a while, and I was getting interested in

what he had to say. But all of a sudden, he asked if I was ready to take off, and he left to go to the restroom. I was only half-finished with my drink. I *hated* not knowing exactly what to do. Should I wait here for him? Find the waitress and pay? Or what?

I waited a minute, and then fished money out of my purse, found the waitress, and paid her. I went outside and met Perry waiting for me.

He volunteered to drive to the park. That was nice, at least. He was parked next to me, so I opened my trunk and got out a cooler.

Perry looked at me. "Oh. Is this going to be a picnic?" Did I detect a bit of a snooty undertone? At least it sounded that way to me.

"Oh, no, don't worry. I just thought I'd pack some bottles of water on ice because it's kind of hot today." I answered him tone for tone. He quickly nodded and thanked me. Then he took the cooler from me and put it in his car.

Once in his car, I quickly forgot that he'd sounded stuck-up. We had a fairly nice conversation, with me asking most of the questions, although he did ask me a lot more than Bernie the "talk-aholic" had. We drove the gravel roads to the Mounds State Preserve, parked the car, and got out. He had come prepared, too. He sprayed mosquito/tick spray on his legs and shoes, and handed me the can. Ah, that was thoughtful!

Then he reached down, rubbed his legs with his hands, and then rubbed his face. Guess I wouldn't have to worry about any kissing today!

We started hiking. Or rather, he did. I was hurrying to keep up with his strides, so I had to alternate between a trot and a sprint once in awhile. I attempted to stay beside him so we could talk some more, when I suddenly noticed the vegetation that I was walking in alongside the trail.

"Hey!" I stopped. "Is this poison ivy?" I asked uncertainly.

"Looks like it to me." He had barely paused to glance at it.

Somehow, I got the feeling he didn't want to deal with anything that would interrupt his hike. Even his date.

"Okey-doke. Guess I'll walk behind you." I felt very much like a female slave walking behind the male owner. At least he couldn't see me stick my tongue out at him.

It turned out to be a good thing I wasn't next to him, though. Then I wasn't in close range to the belches that suddenly began emanating from him after we'd started hiking up a small hill. My definition of a man in a very professional job like Perry's was that manners should be a given. After the third burp without so much as an apology or "excuse me," I felt offended, tapped him on the shoulder, and rather brusquely asked him if his free water at the restaurant had been too spicy.

He looked a little abashed, but didn't say anything, just kept on hiking. When I saw a mosquito land on his back, I told him to hold on a "sec," and took a little bit of delight in slapping the bug a bit harder than I should have. He only thanked me and continued on.

We finished our hike about forty-five minutes later. I

did get to walk beside him for a bit, but I was breathing heavily and panting (from exertion), and very sweaty by the time we got back to the parking lot. Perry suggested we sit at a picnic table and talk. Well, that was nice, I supposed. Maybe there would be some camaraderie after all.

To be grudgingly truthful, because by then I was sure I didn't like this man, we did have an interesting conversation. It ranged from monarch butterflies to Richard M. Nixon. Unfortunately, it also included a rant from Perry about Iowa highway patrolmen who'd had the nerve, evidently, to stop him only because his license plate was out of state. (*He must be a defense attorney*, I thought.) Oh, and he also divulged the fact that he was renting an apartment, and the roommate he'd talked about was a woman.

Really? Do sixty-something men have female roomies? I thought. *Surely he has enough money that he doesn't have to share a residence. Didn't his profile say he had* two *homes, one in this state?* I had assumed that "home" meant a complete "house." I had also assumed that when he said he wasn't looking for a gal pal, he meant a gal who wasn't sharing the same living quarters as he. Apparently I had made several wrong assumptions about this man.

But at that point, I didn't really care. There definitely was *no* chemistry between us, and I was anxious to get home and into my lovely air-conditioned house . . . the house I shared with no one, except Ralphie the dog.

We hopped into Perry's car, and started out on the park's gravel road. I found out why, in all probability, the Iowa highway patrol had stopped Perry: He suddenly became like a sixteen-year-old new driver trying to impress a girl. Was this man going through a second childhood?

Childhood was actually too kind a word. "Grossly immature" would be more descriptive. This man was sixty-four years old, and on the way back into town, he sped. I had no idea someone could burn rubber on gravel, but I was sure I'd heard the squeal of his tires as the rocks and dust flew up! He also kept the windows down in his car. That allowed the wind and dust to complete my totally frazzled look.

I kept my hands on my hair so I wouldn't end up looking like Kramer from *Seinfeld*. I didn't say a word, but only because I didn't want to give Perry the satisfaction of knowing he was scaring the bejeebers out of me. What a jerk! My high-school friends had been right!

He raced into town. Either he was hoping he would bait another trooper and get a ticket so he could sound off on how wronged he was, he was truly showing off to win me over, or he was trying to get the date over with as fast as he could. I suspected it was the latter. At least, that was certainly how I felt!

Somehow, we made it safely back to the parking lot where my car was. I figured he'd rev his engine up while I clambered out of his car, and would then peel out. But he actually turned off the engine, carried my cooler, and walked me over to my car. Then, as if he felt there had to be closure, he said, "Well, maybe we can get together sometime."

"Right," I answered drily. Good thing we weren't in a court of law, sworn to tell the truth.

He turned and walked back to his car. No wave. No handshake. No hug. Not even an attempted kiss. *Really, what a jerk!*

Georgie Porgie

All too soon after the jerk, I had another outdoor date. But this was one I was looking forward to. My Cheesecake Factory friend Dave had kept in touch with me, and we'd discovered we each liked good old-fashioned picnics—truly refreshing to find out after getting the impression some dates didn't care for them. He invited me to one at a state park with a lake, just south of where I lived. He insisted that I not bring anything: He would bring homemade fried chicken, potato salad, regular lettuce salad, some rolls, and dessert. That turned out to be Dove chocolates.

Chocolates! Was this the man of my dreams? I may have been a "good girl" growing up, relatively speaking, but I was not without vices. My vices were a dentist's delight: Anything sweet to the palate was my downfall, and chocolate was the main culprit. The thought of a good old-fashioned picnic sounded like fun. I answered his email request for this date with an eager "I'm in!"

Awww! He really was so sweet! Had any of my other dates treated me this way? *No,* I thought wryly. It sounded like Dave was set to spoil me. For the first time in the years since my husband's sudden death, I felt like I was in heaven.

But one step outside reminded me July could be as hot as "not heaven." I'd begun to wish I hadn't started dating in the heat of summer. I didn't remember the heat and humidity of Iowa summers bothering me when I was sixteen as much as they did now that I was old . . . ish. I duly applied extra deodorant, plastered my hair with heavy-duty hairspray, and used eyeliner guaranteed not to melt in the humidity. I was set.

Dave drove to my house to pick me up. I have no idea if online dating sites have rules that discourage a second date seeing where you live, but how could anyone who loved cheesecake and chocolate not be safe? Calories excluded, that was. From our first date and the ensuing emails we'd shared, I felt comfortable with Dave, so I had no worries at all about him coming to my house.

When he walked up to my door, it was like old home week. I introduced him to Ralphie, who promptly licked his hand. *That's a good sign,* I thought. Even though Ralphie was probably the type of dog who would welcome a burglar into the house and happily give him a tour in exchange for a pat on the head, I still took Ralphie's reaction to Dave as approval.

After some talk about the weather, something which I would encourage all ladies to be an expert on if they want to have something to talk about, Dave walked me to the car and opened the door. Off we drove to the lake for our picnic.

This man Dave had to have been a Boy Scout, because he was totally prepared for everything. He found a beautiful spot with a picnic table overlooking the lake. He fished out a blue-checked tablecloth and spread it on the top of the table. He followed with *real* plates and silverware— he even had wet wipes for me to use to wash my hands after eating that finger-licking-good chicken! I wouldn't have been surprised if he'd pulled out some candles and lit them. All the time we were laughing and talking. It was so pleasant, and the food was delicious. This guy was a gem! It was definitely the perfect date.

And then the *one* cloud with rain floated overhead and decided to cut loose right over our picnic table in the middle of our eating chicken.

My eyeliner was not waterproof. My hairspray failed miserably. The "curls" (frizz or kinks) that appeared when my hair got wet stuck out like devil's horns. But at least Dave had seen me before when I was relatively decent-looking.

Ever since that first date, he'd kept in touch with me through email as a friend. On this date, he was awesome. He kept complimenting me so much, in spite of my being soaked, that I began to think maybe I'd just use him as a gauge of my looks rather than a realistic mirror.

Once the cloudburst was over, we packed up our picnic remnants, and decided to amble down the hill to the lake. It was peaceful and quiet . . . and evidently romantic for my suitor. We held hands, ostensibly in order to help each other stay upright during the downhill trek. But every time I glanced over at him, he was looking at me with his beautiful blue eyes, creased at the sides with laugh-lines. Only he wasn't laughing.

I thought I recognized that look. There's a song about that look. It was "The Look of Love." I began to feel a little nervous, because this was only our second date. We were just friends. I'd thought Dave might be the companion, besides my dog, that my children were anxious for me to have. But was I ready for real romance? I knew I'd grown to feel *fond* of him through our correspondence. And our memorable first-date-that-almost-wasn't was the best date I'd had yet in my electronic-dating quest. This picnic date, in spite of the rain, was so sweet. He was treating me like a queen.

As I continued my downhill trek, I frantically tried to remember how it was when I'd started dating my husband some forty years ago. When did I even begin to get serious? Certainly not on a second date. For heaven's sake, my husband and I had both only been teenagers! I wondered what protocol was at this age.

This age! Hey! I need to remember I am an adult now. Thinking that, I felt less intimidated and worried. *I can handle this guy. We're just friends.* And I had to admit, I was a bit curious and interested in finding out more about this knight-in-polo-shirt-and-shorts.

At the foot of the hill, we stood and looked at the lake for about two minutes, which was about a minute longer than needed to watch water. Then we headed back up the hill. If there truly was any romance in the air, it began to fade quickly—as quickly as our stamina faded as we both struggled for breath.

The hill was a lot easier going down than it was coming back up. He was sweating, I was panting, and it had nothing to do with love! My hip started hurting, too, and I kept my fingers crossed that I wouldn't start wheezing or pass out from the exertion. Another inopportune reminder I wasn't sixteen anymore.

Finally we made it, still holding hands for support. It took a few minutes for us to catch our breath, and we finally were able to laugh at how out of shape we were. When Dave suggested that we go for a drive, I was on board!

Iowa in the summer can be so picturesque, especially from the inside of an air-conditioned car. No mosquitoes, no flies, and no humidity! I knew Dave was watching me as I fussed with my hair in the passenger-side mirror, so I started talking. At least with this date, there was no need to worry about the four-second-silence rule—my Cheesecake Factory guy was full of jokes and quips, and loved music. He had all my favorite CDs in his car, so the drive was actually a lot of fun!

The more we talked, the more we discovered how much we had in common, too. What particularly impressed me were his stories of how he'd raised his third child, his little girl, after his wife had died from cancer. Yet, with him, the glass was always half full in life. I could talk to him about being a widow and how much death had affected my life and not think that I was boring him. Then a song started playing on one of the CDs, and he burst into a totally off-key rendition of it. I giggled like a kid, and was totally enchanted. I could laugh with ease with this dear friend.

As we headed around a corner, I told him that there was a nature center up ahead if he wanted to see that. He pulled the car into the entrance parking lot, and we ended up walking to a quiet spot with lots of wildflowers and prairie grasses.

The sun was setting, and a light breeze blew my hair back into some semblance of what I had originally styled it to be. We were holding hands, just like two little kids. We paused near a sculpture of a buffalo, and we alternated between looking at it and smiling at each other.

I began to wonder just how this was going to end. We couldn't stand there and smile all the time, could we? But I enjoyed this date, and maybe it was time to bite the bullet and give him a friendly little thank-you kiss. Remembering what I'd said to him after our first date, I blurted out, "Well, shall we see if there are any romantic sparks now?" Brilliant!

It was as though I'd fired a starter's pistol. Dave didn't answer—he was too busy pulling me to him, and he kissed me. It was nice and sweet, just like him. I looked into his beautiful blue eyes and smiled. He smiled back and then he kissed me again. How do I describe this second kiss? Well, hungry would do it. Like what a sugar-holic might feel after being on a diet for a week and then being handed a plateful of cookies. Only it wasn't me who was hungry—*he* was!

If this had been a romantic movie, I'd have melted into his arms and kissed him back as passionately as I could remember how. (And I didn't think I could remember!). But instead, I had a most unromantic reaction: I started crying! Crying as hard as if he'd slapped my face. Crying as hard as when I had been told several years earlier that my husband had died of sudden death syndrome. But those tears had been shed in shock and grief. These tears were the result of horrible guilt and fear. I don't know why, unless it was because we'd just been talking about our departed spouses, but I felt like I had just *cheated* on my husband, and I felt absolutely terrified of the feelings I'd stirred up in my date!

Poor dear Dave was horrified. He must have thought he'd accidentally bitten me! I don't know. Both of us kept apologizing profusely as we got back into the car and drove to my house.

I was miserable. I figured with all the tears, sniffling, and hiccupping I was doing, Dave was either going to be worried about the water-repellency of his upholstery, or afraid he was going to catch some sort of upper respiratory infection. I felt doubly bad—I had spoiled a perfectly nice get-together with a true gentleman who was (or had been) fond of me, and I'd made a blubbering mess of myself in the process. And for what, I couldn't find the words to explain.

What was *wrong* with me? Did I suffer from Georgie Porgie syndrome? Dave jokingly said he'd never kissed a girl and made her cry before! He was trying to make me feel better, but I only felt more wretched that he was being so nice. He patted my shoulder, shushed me, and told me seriously that he knew exactly what I was going through. He'd been widowed longer than I had been, he said, and he selflessly took the blame for rushing things. Before I slunk into my house, we decided to part ways, at least for a while.

Since confession is sometimes good for the soul, I told a good friend about what had happened to me. I was debating whether or not I was really ready to continue this online-dating adventure. Her words of advice? "Well, Beck, you know what they say, if you fall off a horse—you pick yourself up, dust yourself off, and get right back on!"

Okay, maybe. But I still wasn't sure I wanted to put myself back into a situation where I might hurt someone's feelings. Or mine. I just needed to get Dave and the crying jag out of my mind. *Maybe,* I thought, *I need to go shopping. I need a hobby.*

Well, my new hobby of cyber-dating might get my mind on other things. I hoped I'd learned my lesson with not only my feelings, but also those of my date. I'd just have to stay away from romantic spots. Or start reading every romance novel I could to get some pointers on how to behave!

Automatic Amore

If there's one thing I've noticed all of us "oldsters" have in common, it's that we quickly get into habits. It doesn't matter what the habit is—there are as many different kinds of habits as there are people—but everyone has at least one. I had an embarrassing incident with one of my dates because of an unrecognized habit that I had.

I was driving home early one evening from visiting my parents when my cell phone rang. I normally don't answer when I'm driving, but this dating thing had made a lot of abnormal behavior on my part seem normal, so I answered. It was a surprise call from "Big Bad John," alias the guy whose name I couldn't keep straight. He explained he had driven the two and a half hours from his home to Des Moines to visit a relative. He was done with that, and wondered if he could see me.

I immediately slowed to a crawl, and told him I was in the car and could meet him somewhere. He said he knew where the casino was, if I didn't mind going there. My last time being at the casino with the Ebenezer Scrooge clone had grossed me out, but I told Big Bad John I'd meet him there. I was tempted to tell him to be sure not to have any drinks, in case he was anything like the toilet bowl gold-digger, but the odds against that happening again had to be enormous, I hoped.

I pulled a U-turn and drove back to the city. I stopped a block from my rendezvous to grab my makeup bag, spent five minutes fussing over trying to make one strand of hair lie straight, and then pulled up in the corner of the large casino parking lot, where BBJ was already parked.

I was actually glad I would see Big Bad John again. After the first date, we had progressed from more emails to telephone calls, since he lived so far away. I loved talking to him because he was actually funny, had a lot of stories to tell, and was very intelligent.

But I guess I had forgotten what he really looked like, because after he heaved his big frame out of a surprisingly little car and smiled down at me, I saw he had a dimple. I hadn't really noticed that at the restaurant on our first date. It was adorable, and I'm a sucker for dimples. I was relieved he didn't give me a hello kiss. After the Georgie Porgie incident, I had sworn off kissing for a while, and was proud of myself that I no longer fantasized about kissing in the mirror--that had been *way* too much work.

We talked while we walked indoors. He asked if I'd like to play a slot machine. I never had before, so I said I'd just watch him. Just in case his luck was as big as he was, I offered to split any winnings with him. He didn't comment on that, because he was obviously distracted by, or attracted to, a machine that featured a picture of a very busty and scantily clad woman in a very suggestive pirate outfit. The flashing neon lights beckoned players to enjoy finding her "treasure chest."

Oh, brother! Leave it to a guy to pick that one. Big Bad John sat down to play. Over all the noise of the beeps, clangs, and buzzes from the various slot machines, I hollered into his ear that someone had once told me that I was a pirate's dream: I had a sunken chest.

I expected him to laugh at that old joke, but he just flashed his dimple in a grin as he looked at my bosom for a second. Then he shook his head, and began pulling the slot machine's handle. I looked down at my chest to see if what I'd said was true.

The pirate lady's treasure chest remained unopened as he blew twenty bucks on the slots in just a few minutes. He announced he was quitting, and we should find a quiet place to visit. He was retired, so naturally we grabbed *free* pop and *free* coffee and sat at a table overlooking the racetrack. We talked . . . and laughed . . . and talked . . . and bantered back and forth. We even made a date for the Iowa State Fair that would be in Des Moines in a few weeks.

Soon it was getting dark and almost past bedtime. It was nine p.m., and Big Bad John still had a two-hour drive to make. We hurried back out to the parking lot and continued talking until we said goodbye. A beautiful full moon hung over the racetrack and casino building. I gave him a hug and turned my head quickly so that he brushed his lips on my cheek instead of my lips. No way was I going to risk another mouth-to-mouth kiss by anyone!

I slid into my car and fumbled for my keys, while he

stood next to me to make sure I got off safely. I don't know if it was the moon that made me act like a lunatic, or just what possessed me. I didn't even look at him, but said, "Good night. Love you!"

AACCKK! I realized what I'd said immediately as I said it. I clapped my hands to my mouth so fast my teeth hurt. Mother of GAWD, where had that come from? I looked up at Big Bad John in horror. What would he think of me saying that after only our second date? It made Dave's second date kiss seem like a pat on the head, compared to someone blurting out to a guy that she *loves* him! I couldn't talk fast enough to apologize and hoped he didn't take me seriously. This was only the second time I'd seen him, and both times had ended with my cheeks burning in humiliation. His dimple was getting a workout—he was laughing at me. He kindly said there were all sorts of love!

Oh, gee whiz, what did *that* mean? The last time BBJ had said something to me, I'd analyzed and fretted over the meaning until I had almost ruined my bathroom mirror!

So I yelled at him as he got into his car, "I mean—Like you a lot!" Maybe that would negate the error.

The entire way home, I agonized over having a big mouth that I couldn't control. All I could come up with for an excuse was that, when I say good night on the phone to my mom, my dad, my daughters, the grandkids, my siblings, my cousins, or any dear friends, I always say "Good night! Love you!" Guess it was just a habit.

Until this happened, I hadn't realized how often I said it. Maybe "love you" had become another synonym for "goodbye." Since I'm too old to break most of my habits, I should probably prepare myself for someday telling the grocery store clerk or the guy who changes my oil, "Love you!"

As soon as I got home, I posted this gaffe on Facebook. I thought maybe publicly confessing my humiliation would erase it. But I was pleasantly surprised at all the confessions I received from my cyber friends after they read my post. Evidently I was *not* the only one with the habit of telling people I love them. Various friends of mine had accidentally given the verbal Valentine to an attorney, the Sears dryer installer, and the dog groomer, to name a few.

Ah! I felt so much better. Then I had to write: *Love you, Facebook friends!*

Winks

There were several cutesy little terms on the dating site. You could "like" someone, mark someone as "favorite," and/or "wink." "Like" meant you'd glanced at this profile and were interested. "Favorite" meant out of all the profiles, this one was the best. And "wink" was just like the real thing—a way to flirt.

Only in the world of electronic dating can you get hit on without ever meeting the guy. I found the "winks" annoying at first because they piqued my curiosity. I would have to go into the guy's profile, check him out, and see just where and from whence the wink originated. Quite often it was from someone in another state. I wasn't going to respond to anyone who was too far away to help me empty a mousetrap (with the exception of Big Bad John).

This was when I missed the good ol' days of in-person contact. When a guy winked at me then, I could immediately tell if it was because he was letting me in on a joke (wink, accompanied by a slight grin), if he was flirting with me (wink, accompanied by a seductive smile or attempt thereof), or if he just had something in his eye (a long wink, accompanied by a grimace and maybe tears). Yes, I certainly preferred the genuine article . . . and evidently one of my dates did, too. Only I didn't mean it.

✒︎

Part of this new life of dating meant I had to try different makeup. It was an unwritten, personal law unto myself—I *had* to try stuff. I tried it in an unsuccessful and vain effort to thwart aging, but also because after having watched my two daughters try on all sorts of junk as they grew up, I finally had my turn. I *like* to put makeup on. Maybe I should have been a clown.

It was kind of fun to experiment with different shades of lipstick, eyeliner, shadow, foundation, and blush. But mascara has always been a staple of mine. I always used mascara because, until recent medical inventions, it was the best way to plump up my skinny little eyelashes. My eyelashes were the only thing classified as "hair" that did not get thicker during my aging process. One ad for mascara promised consumers they could have lashes that looked like they came from using a prescription, but without the doctor's appointment and cost. Sold! I could hardly wait to use the product. I imagined just how fuller and thicker lashes would accent and brighten my eyes.

I had a date coming up, a real date in the evening at a nice restaurant. About an hour before we met, I put on at least three applications of my new mascara, stuck the tube in my purse in case I needed to touch up later, and headed out to the restaurant.

We had a pleasant conversation and a delicious meal. This gentleman was a little shy, but very nice. However, I wasn't getting any vibes that he found me exciting. I was even beginning to think I was just a warm body so that he didn't have to eat alone. Maybe it wouldn't hurt to vamp myself up a bit. I excused myself to the ladies' room to freshen up.

Freshening up is something everyone over the age of forty should take advantage of, because gravity affects not only the body, but the makeup, too. It tends to head south, and I didn't want black eyes or lips that looked like they were bleeding. Good thing I checked everything. Another few minutes and my date would have looked like he was courting someone greatly into Goth looks. I reapplied my lip plumper (not that it worked), my lipstick, and lip gloss. I grabbed a handful of toilet paper and wiped a ton of black eyeliner off from under my eyes, then carefully relined them. Finally I freshened my mascara with one more coat. Done!

Before I left the ladies' room, I studied myself in the mirror and decided that my right eyelashes didn't seem as thick as the left ones. Easy fix—I simply applied another coat of my new mascara. It still didn't look right, so I touched the tips of my lashes with the wand.

Another minute later, I had put on two more coats of mascara on each eye, and I could swear my eyes felt a little heavy. One more look in the mirror, though, and wow! I looked great—at least a whole year younger.

Back at the table, we resumed talking over dessert.

Suddenly, my nose itched, and I sneezed. Nothing major—just a nice little feminine *ah-choo*. But as I raised my head to smile at my date for saying, "Bless you," the heavily coated lashes on my right eye stuck together like Velcro. It was only for a second, but it was long enough that it looked like a wink.

I glanced at my date to see if he'd noticed. He had. But he'd misinterpreted the makeup malfunction. He winked back at me. Oops! Should I confess, or just smile and hope it didn't happen again?

I took a chance that the lashes were now free, and tried holding my eyes open longer than normal to give the lashes a chance to really dry. My date seemed very encouraged by my wide-eyed look, and probably thought I was looking amazed at whatever story it was that he was telling. If he'd had plumage, he'd have started preening himself.

Truthfully, I had no idea what he was talking about, because I was concentrating on my eyes. I was going to have to blink soon, or they would tear up, my makeup would run down my face, and I'd end up looking like a reject from the music group KISS. Oh, dear. So I blinked, which felt good, but also gave the lashes in my *left* eye their turn to stick together.

What the heck was going on? By this time, my date seemed impressed that my eyelids were ambidextrous. He tried to wink back with his other eye, all the while telling me some story. Like a very slow-motion game of tennis, we volleyed winks back and forth. I finally kept my head down and looked at my lap because if I looked at him,

I was afraid the rest of the date would be nothing but a winkfest.

I was so annoyed with myself. I tried casually pulling at the bottom lashes of one eye to work off some of the caked-on mascara, all the while trying to carry on a conversation. But it was as though the mascara had turned into beauty spackle. It was at least hardening enough that my winking wasn't so constant. Thank heaven, dessert was over, my date was looking at his watch, and we could get ready to leave!

My gentleman came to my side to pull my chair out for me. How nice! As I stood up, though, I started to sneeze again, and squeezed both eyes tightly shut. Darn! Both eyes stuck closed. Darn again! I couldn't see for a second whether or not I'd sneezed on anything. I quickly raised my face up in the hopes that my lashes would follow suit, separate, and open up, too. No luck.

I felt my date's body as I bumped into him. What did he think of me? Probably that I was a klutz. Finally, both my eyes flew open just in time to see my date's face in front of me, lips pursed for a smooch! He must have thought I was waiting to be kissed! Oh, my goodness! This was a public place.

What should I do in a situation like this? The whole thing was so ridiculous that I started to giggle. He drew back with a puzzled look on his face, but was good-natured enough to smile. All I could do was shake my head, and start walking in front of him out of the restaurant.

When I finally got to my car, I confessed my narcissistic

sin, and we both had a good laugh. Then I got a real kiss, but there were no sparks. Just another crazy date for me.

Bad Boyz

One morning when I checked my online-dating emails, I discovered that one man and I were a 97 percent match! His profile picture showed a nice-looking man with dark hair and a mustache, rather lean and with a broad and bright smile on his face. He had a wonderful profile. Another one of his pictures was with his two young adult children—both college graduates and nice-looking. He wrote with a sense of humor. I liked that.

And he was divorced. Twice. And had just ended a long relationship. I didn't think I liked that! I had to read it again, because that seemed like more baggage than I wanted to handle. How could something that major count as only 3 percent of our nonmatching?

But for some reason, I continued to read more about him. The more I read, the better he actually sounded. I began to wonder if the divorces and breakup weren't his fault. It would be the kind thing to do to give him the benefit of the doubt. It must have been Fate, because later in the afternoon that I read about him, he sent me an email saying he'd never gotten a 97 percent match before. If I wasn't already seeing anyone, he wrote, would I like to correspond with him for a bit?

Would I? This guy was exactly on the same wavelength as I was. We started exchanging emails almost as fast as one was read.

Our similarities were amazing. He'd grown up on a farm just fifteen miles south of my hometown. A flurry of emails followed where we each talked about our hometowns and subsequent places we lived.

Like me, he was the oldest of six children. He only had one sister and the rest were brothers, but we'd had the same problems being the oldest and having to live with younger sibs. It appeared that both sets of our parents must have been simultaneously telling us that we were the role models and had to set good examples for the younger family members! Geesh!

His favorite pet had been his pony. (Could this get any better?)

Yes, it could. He owned his own business, and his income was "comfortable." Not that being rich was my number one priority in a date, but it certainly wouldn't hurt.

We both liked looking at clouds and stargazing. We both seemed to have the same values, not counting the number of marriages. This was fun, having a fairly rapid-fire conversation through email. Reading them, re-reading them, I couldn't believe how lucky I was to have "almost" met a guy who seemed to be so perfect in so many ways. Hey, this electronic match-up stuff really did work!

I was intrigued. And then he started to flirt with me. Oh, the advantages of email! I could scrutinize each one he sent me and answer him back in kind, I hoped! Sometimes I just used the smiley-face emoticon, or maybe the winking one. Cleverness had never flowed so easily from my fingertips to a keyboard before. He was on a roll, too. His emails were gentle little flirtations that I printed off and saved as carefully as if they were love letters.

He thought I was the most beautiful woman he'd ever seen. I confessed that my picture was three years old—but hastened to assure him that my children swore I hadn't changed a bit! He confessed he was trying to break a smoking habit and was afraid he would succeed only if someone kicked him in the behind. I volunteered.

After about twenty-five emails back and forth, we both noticed it was getting late, so he signed off with a final email for the day: "Me and Becky sitting in a tree, K-I-S-S-I-N-G . . . "

I must have been worn out from all the emails, because normally I would have looked at that, thought, "What a weirdo!" and gone on to the next possible date. Instead, I was enchanted. No man had ever written me a poem before, even a cheesy take on a children's taunt. This man was nostalgic, sentimental, and sweet.

I've heard through the years that too much time on a computer can damage brain cells. Studies have apparently shown that as humans age, our brain cells begin to die. Studies have shown constant exposure to chemicals (as in hair dyes) may cause brain cell damage. I was three for three on the brain-damage scale. I was pathetically doomed. Or crazy. *Totally demented,* the small part of my brain that was still functioning normally said. Nah—I banished those thoughts immediately and went with the nostalgic, sentimental, and sweet ones. I should have listened to myself.

The next day was much the same. Back and forth we typed to each other. I started to remember hearing how people fall madly in love before ever meeting in person because they are captivated by each other through writing. Wasn't that the way the writers Elizabeth Barrett Browning and Robert Browning had met? Wouldn't that be awesome if someday this man and I were on a commercial for electronic dating, telling about how we fell in love before we even met, thanks to cyberspace?

Like the ads on TV that show a normal person and the same person as a creepy alter ego, I became normal "me" and creepy juvenile "me." That's how addicted I became to all these emails. I realized I needed to take a deep breath and slow down. I needed to get back to work, for heaven's sake—my office break had been over fifteen minutes ago! So I told my email suitor I needed to close down for a while. He apologized, and told me he really needed to get back to work, too. Ten minutes later—ding! Another email from him. He missed me, he said, and he hadn't even met me!

It was like passing notes in a classroom. I felt like I

was sixteen again—and I hoped the teacher didn't catch me wasting time that didn't belong to me. Feeling guilty for looking at personal email after my break had ended, I worked extra through lunch. Sin was cleansed!

At home, I had my computer all to myself, and he had his, too. After we'd been emailing each other for four days, he gave me his phone number, and asked if I would like to meet him the coming weekend. Of course! In my reply, I gave him my full name, and asked what his last name was. He responded with suggestions of what to do on a Sunday afternoon, all sweet and all sounding like a wonderful first date. It was my choice, so I picked a meeting at a park and an early dinner afterward, and then asked for his last name again, in case (like my Cheesecake Factory date), something were to come up.

Again, I got a chatty email. We bantered back and forth, and then it was time for bed and a sign-off for the day. As I got ready for bed, it occurred to me that he hadn't told me his last name, even though I'd asked for it at least three times. As Scooby Doo would say, "Ruh-roh!" But maybe he'd just been so excited that he'd missed that part of my email. So I went to sleep. I'd just email him again in the morning.

One thing that was not on my profile, and that I don't make a habit of telling my prospective dates, was that I was a worrier. I worried about the weather. I worried about getting to places on time. I worried about my kids, my grandkids, my job, world peace—you name it, I've worried about it.

So it was not unusual for me to wake up constantly through that night worried that this 97 percent match was too good to be true. That last name omission was a red flag—heaven knows that in all the Googling I'd done while participating in this kind of dating, I'd read plenty of warnings about what to watch out for to protect oneself. While it would have been easy to dismiss it, failure to answer a direct question was one of the warnings.

The first thing I did in the morning was fire up my computer and pretend I was a teenage Nancy Drew. Yes, everything would be fine, I was sure, but so that I would quit worrying, I would do some actual sleuthing—just like my childhood heroine!

The adult me was soon thrilled to discover that I could do a "reverse phone number" check. Aha! Here was my date! And his last name. Next step was to Google him, and . . .

Hooray! He *was* who he said he was! He was a businessman, he was on professional sites, he was a Chamber of Commerce member, and woo-hoo! He was rich! A six-figure income! Phew! I guessed if I had an income that large, I wouldn't want strangers to know how rich I was, either. At that point, I was so relieved that my new friend was legitimate that it wouldn't have mattered if he were a pauper. My worries were for naught.

I was just about to sign off to get ready for work, when

I noticed his name in another article down at the very bottom of the page. I scrolled down, clicked on it . . . and there he was.

Only this time he wasn't smiling or looking directly at the camera. Either he was the world's worst dresser, or that was an orange prison jumpsuit he was wearing! It took me an instant to realize the blackboard in his hands, with a series of numbers on it, meant jail. It was a mugshot.

Holy Schnikeys! Could I have been murdered? I have found in my "older" age that I can no longer ride roller coasters, tilt-a-whirls, or other fast and crazy rides like that, because I get dizzy and sick to my stomach. That's exactly how I felt looking at that mugshot—totally sick. Forget 97 percent similarities! That terrible 3 percent trumped everything. I read the article over and over again until it sunk in. It seemed that the almost-perfect date had been arrested for domestic abuse. Well, what did I expect from someone who wrote such *stupid poetry*! At least it wasn't murder, but . . . I began to get mad and madder, until I was so furious at almost being duped that I wondered what *I'd* look like in an orange jumpsuit—after being booked for manslaughter.

Then there was the matter of this picture. The mugshot, taken about nine months ago, was of a graying, scraggly-faced guy. While he still looked a little like the profile picture, he had to be at least fifteen, maybe twenty years older than the profile picture I'd been gazing at in adoration for almost a week. Now I thought of him with disgust and as some career criminal. Maybe like Clyde Barrow of *Bonnie and Clyde* fame. Idiot me! Well, as the saying goes, "Hell hath no fury like a woman scorned." I had almost been conned. What did this guy, Clyde, think I was? Stupid, obviously. Well, he was right.

A million ways to teach Clyde a lesson raced through my mind. Confrontation chicken that I am, it took me about half an hour to screw up enough courage to actually do something. I finally picked up the phone and dialed his number.

A rather high, strained voice answered on the other end. I couldn't tell if it was male or female.

"Uh, hi, Becky?" He had my phone number from a few days ago, so I knew he must have caller ID. He sounded nervous and scared. Maybe that's why his voice was high.

I took a big breath and said: "Was there something you wanted to tell me before our date this weekend?"

"Oh."

Yes, "oh." That said it all. Clyde never apologized, but just started a lengthy explanation, starting with saying he'd wanted to tell me his past in person, on our date coming up. *Wouldn't that have been nice, getting hit with that bombshell in public?* I thought.

He'd had a relationship with a woman for five years—he'd told me that in an earlier email—but, he explained, he hadn't known she was an alcoholic. She would get drunk, steal things from him, and get into fights with him that she instigated. One night he kicked her out, and then when he left his house, she came back drunker than ever. She had fallen in the house, and called the police, claiming that he had abused her. Why, he whined to me on the phone, even the police who arrested him didn't believe her.

He was innocent! The case was even dismissed without prejudice, which meant, he told me, that he was cleared! He would even give me his case number and I could check it out myself. To be truthful, I had already "checked out"— as soon as I'd heard his whiny voice. Maybe this mugshot was a blessing. But I played along.

"Okay," I said, "what's the number?" If he was bluffing, I was mad enough to call him on it.

He gave it to me. Then he said his picture shouldn't even be public, and the only reason it was on the web was because some firm that posts mugshots of anyone who is arrested—innocent or not—demands a ridiculous amount of money to get it off the Internet, and he wasn't going to pay it. A six-figure income, and he'd rather let his reputation be ruined than pay a hundred bucks? "Mr. Perfect" not only wasn't perfect; he had poor taste, he was cheap, and he was a liar.

I told him I'd check out his story and get back to him, then hung up. As soon as I quit shaking, I thought, *Now what?* Checking out some probable criminal's claim was way outside my comfort zone. Thanks to Google, however, I found out just how easy it was to do.

Clyde's story was partially true. He'd only spent one night in jail, was released on his own recognizance, and the charges were indeed dismissed without prejudice. But "without prejudice" didn't mean what Clyde told me it meant. After checking with a relative of mine who was also an attorney, I found that "dismissed without prejudice" means the person whose case it is (Clyde) can be tried again.

This time I emailed Clyde. Short, sweet, and to the point: **_Goodbye._** I almost added, *And, by the way, you're a high talker and your profile picture looks stupid.* (I am a teensy bit ashamed that I wanted to resort to name calling as though I were some angry child, but it felt good at the time, and I *had* been acting like an immature juvenile.)

Two weeks later, I was curious to see if this little incident had had any effect on him. His profile was gone and he was no longer on the site. Maybe I'd saved some other poor women from thinking Clyde was Mr. Perfect. When I started writing this book, I double-checked him again. There he was—same picture, same profile. But obviously he'd never found a ladylove.

You know, feeling smug can be a good sensation.

The Old Gray Mare, She Ain't What She Used to Be

I *love* horses. Always have, always will. I am one of those lucky kids who actually got my own pony. When I was ten, my dad was transferred to another town just twenty miles away from where we were currently living. Today, people commute hours and miles away from where they actually live. But back then, at least with my dad's company, the family had to be as close as possible to where he worked. My folks couldn't find any place in the new town that suited them, so for almost a year, we rented a farm outside the town where Dad had to work. A *farm*! I was in horse heaven.

I had read every book ever written about horses: Walter Farley's *Black Stallion* series, everything Marguerite Henry wrote, and Mary Elwyn Patchett's *Brumby* books. I even wrote to the Chincoteague Fire Department after I read Henry's *Misty of Chincoteague*, and received a beautiful card and letter from the fire chief himself! Saturday mornings would find me glued to the TV watching *My Friend Flicka* and *Fury*. When my family would visit my grandparents, I would beg to go to Uncle Nick and Aunt Joyce's farm. They had quarter horses they would let me ride, and later had two beautiful Paso Fino horses. To ride these animals was like gliding on air, their gaits were so smooth. I wanted a horse of my own so badly that it was always on the top of my Christmas list, and it was the only thing I would wish for whenever I blew out my birthday candles.

The first thing my parents did when we moved to the farm was to find me a stocky, shaggy little Shetland pony. I named him Midnight. He was clever in knowing by the look in my eyes when he was going to be ridden, and would make a mad dash to the other end of the pasture. If I was on him more than thirty minutes, he would get bored and crane his neck around to nip at my bare legs. I rode him bareback, and in the spring when he started shedding, my jeans would look as though they were made of mohair after I slid off his back. He was ornery, mean, and messy—and I loved him dearly!

My parents were pleasantly surprised at how I took care of little Middy. I hauled buckets of water down to his stall in the winter, cleaned up after him, and brushed him constantly. I rode Midnight around and around, daydreaming of being a princess astride a huge Budweiser-type Clydesdale riding behind a chivalrous knight. When I saw an old rerun on TV of young Elizabeth Taylor in *National Velvet* riding a horse in a famous steeplechase, Midnight became my jumper. I thrilled to the feeling of him gathering up his four stubby little legs and leaping across a foot-wide creek that dribbled through our pasture.

When I had filled out my profile, I mentioned I'd had a pony when I was ten and liked riding horses. I didn't mention that the last time I'd ridden was around age thirty, back when my spine had some cushion to it and my legs could grip the horse's barrel and not remain bowed when I got off. But this little tidbit of information about riding evidently caught the eye of one of my potential dates. He emailed me that he enjoyed seeing my picture, I was lovely, smart, et cetera . . . and that he loved horses, too. Whoa, Nelly! I had to take a closer look at this potential match.

His picture was pleasant. He was my age, had a receding hairline of what looked like graying dark hair, a strong jaw, a nice smile, and a straight nose with a mustache that reminded me of Tom Selleck. Hmm. He passed on the "looks" criteria!

He'd had some college. Good. Had grown up in a small town in northeastern Iowa. Great. Father of two adults, grandfather of two little girls. Hey—we had some things in common, for sure. Recently divorced. (Who could divorce a lover of horses?) He was still employed, but looking forward to retirement to travel, probably when he turned sixty-five. He loved to go to movies and read, and enjoyed going to five-star restaurants. And there was the "loves horses" part. This guy I had to meet.

I immediately fired off an email. By now, pro that I'd become at this electronic-dating thing, I had a standard paragraph that I merely copied and pasted. I added that my hometown was a small town, talked about how much we had in common, and ended by saying that I was an experienced horsewoman. I hit "Send" before I wondered if I should have clarified the "experienced horsewoman" description as something that I was in my youth. *Well,* I argued with my conscience, *I do have experience, it was with horses, and I'm a woman, so I guess that's the truth. Maybe this guy used to have horses, and we'll have that fun part of our lives in common.*

Next morning, I turned on the computer, and there were more matches. And a reply from the guy who loved horses. My fingers flew across the computer keys faster than a ticket holder cashing in on a win. My eyes scanned his message. He thought I sounded nice. He thought we had a lot in common. He would like to go horseback riding with me. Would tomorrow (Saturday) morning work? His name was Cal. His phone number was . . .

Wow! A date! And he's obviously in good enough shape to still ride. Oh, but am I? Horseback riding at *my* age? I hadn't been on a horse in years. What if I couldn't remember how to do it? But, gee, if this guy—I'd call him Cowboy Cal, I decided—was my age and still rode, then, yes, I was going to gamble that I wouldn't make a fool of myself.

I called him. He sounded as pleasant as he looked. My heart was beating fast, but I did mention the fact that it had been a "couple" of years since I'd had time to ride. He laughed and said he could say the same thing. I immediately felt better. Cal told me a friend of his recommended a riding stable just south of the city. Would I like to meet there, have a ride, and then maybe go for a late lunch somewhere? I agreed, hung up, and then picked up the phone again.

I made a quick call to the stables, where a tired-sounding woman assured me that they had nice, quiet horses and the ride would be with a large group led by one of her employees. Phew! That sounded nice and safe!

Saturday arrived hot and humid as usual. I debated whether I should spritz on some kind of cool, citrusy perfume, but decided the *eau d'equine* smells around a stable probably wouldn't mix well with that. I popped in my contacts, grabbed my sunglasses, hit my hair with hairspray, and wondered for a millisecond if I should spray on bug repellent. I dismissed that thought, and hopped into the car for my first-ever date with a horse . . . and rider.

For once, I had a date beat me to the venue. As soon as I had parked my car, I spotted a guy who pretty much matched his profile picture striding over to me. Man! I couldn't help smiling. He had a cowboy hat on! What is it about a guy dressed like the Marlboro ad man that sends shivers down women's spines? He wasn't stooped over, or overly paunchy. Cowboy Cal, with that rugged hat and Tom Selleck mustache, actually looked kind of good, as a matter of fact! I just knew we were going to hit it off.

As he got closer, I noticed him kind of looking me up and down. Instinctively, I sucked my stomach in and lifted my head—not in an arrogant, confident way, but more for my turkey neck with the double chin to not be so noticeable. I was wearing jeans, and I was sure the area once called a waist, but now referred to as the ubiquitous muffin-top, was expanding. I tried to stand taller and suck in my stomach harder.

I flashed him what I hoped was a dazzling smile. I was not wearing a cowboy hat, or any type of headgear at all, because I sure didn't want to ruin my hairdo. And I'd stupidly taken off my sunglasses so he could see my lovely blue eye shadow. But I wished I had something on that shaded my face. My smile wasn't the only thing dazzling— the darned sun was so bright that as I looked up at Cowboy Cal, my squinting eyes teared up at the blinding light. Dang it! This was not the way I'd envisioned making a first impression. I took a second to pull myself together, wiped my wet eyes, sidled over a bit so the sun wasn't assaulting me directly in the face, and we introduced ourselves.

I had my old tennies on because I didn't want to step in anything gushy, like, uh, horse apples. He had on what looked like brand-new cowboy boots. I wished I had something else to wear, but I wasn't going to change my shoes to the sandals I had in the car for our after-riding lunch date. But Cal didn't seem to notice my feet. He took my elbow and led me to the front of the stable, where a throng of obviously inexperienced would-be riders had gathered. City slickers, all of us! I wouldn't stand out at all if I couldn't remember how to ride. Cowboy Cal was certainly the most authentic-looking rider there. But not for long.

The first thing all the riders were instructed to do was

don protective headgear that looked like a cross between old football helmets and children's bike helmets. (There went my hairdo.) We all looked more like we were participants in a Roller Derby than riders of horses. I noticed that there were several women who were dressed in tennis shoes, and also had muffin-tops, so thrown together with these matching helmets, I didn't feel so obvious as a nonrider. (*Which*, I told myself, *isn't true, because I* used *to ride!*)

I was ready to mount up and get to riding next to my date. This would be fun! We could amble along the trail and visit, discussing a variety of topics and getting to know each other.

An employee of the stable began leading the horses out one at a time, and handed the reins to each prospective rider to hang on to. I remarked casually that I hoped to get the only palomino there that I had spotted. Not only was it pretty, but I'd been observing how docile it was. It barely moved. The stable hand must have heard me, because he led my very own "Trigger" over to me, and I almost started clapping! This was going to be a piece of cake.

Cowboy Cal was given a big rangy-looking horse, who stood quietly next to mine. I walked closer to my horse, one palm outstretched so the horse would smell me. Trigger, having discovered the open palm did not contain a sugar cube, apple slice, or bit of hay, lowered his head even more, shifted his weight to one side, and stood there. I continued petting his nose, rubbed his face between his eyes, and scratched behind his ears. If any of that felt good to him, he never let me know.

Next from our leader came a quick verbal lesson, followed by an example of how to mount, dismount, and turn the horse's head with the reins, followed by a command for everyone to mount up. I stood by the left side of my horse's saddle, reins in my hand, also grasping the saddle horn. I remembered how to mount! I was so proud of myself, especially when I noticed some of the other riders trying to mount their horse from the right-hand side! They must not have been paying attention to the lessons. I snorted. *Everyone* knows you go from the left!

I then turned to see if Cal was coming to give me a leg up into the saddle. When I saw he was already up in his saddle looking down at me, I gave a little wave, turned to put my left foot in the stirrup, and . . .

Uh-oh, something was wrong here. Why was this stirrup so high? I put a little oomph into swinging my knee up higher so my foot would hit the stirrup, but it only swung down to the ground faster than it had gone up. Oh, dear! "Darn it!" I muttered.

I tried again, but this time my knee swung into the side of poor Trigger's ribcage, and he whipped his head around to give me *THE LOOK*. I gave him what I hoped a horse would know is an "I'm sorry and really didn't mean it" look back. Cal, in an attempt to be helpful that I found annoying, finally spoke up and suggested I adjust the stirrup—if I needed to.

Uh-oh. Did I remember how to do that? My mind was blank! But I rallied. After all, I had recently learned how to adjust my baby granddaughter's car seat, so how hard could this be? I fumbled a bit, and then, thank heaven, the stirrup came down a couple of notches. I shot a look of smug triumph over my shoulder, not knowing if Cal even saw, managed to get my foot in the stirrup, and swung up. My left thigh shot searing swords of pain throughout my whole body. But by gum, I had managed to not only remember how to adjust the stirrup, but get about fifty pounds more of me up in the air than I'd ever had to do when I was sixteen.

Right then, the helper appeared to see if I needed any help. I proudly told him nope, and he moved off, leaving me sitting there with my left side with the stirrup the correct length next to Cal. I smiled over at him, all the while debating whether or not I should call the helper back so that he could adjust the *other* stirrup: the one with my right knee at a ninety-degree angle to my now-screaming right hip. Maybe I could just ease my foot out of the stirrup and let it hang down.

I started a conversation with Cal so he wouldn't notice my extraction efforts. It took me awhile, but finally I was free of pain, and my right leg hung limply next to the very high stirrup.

The worst was over. I was comfortably seated on a horse that had somehow grown taller when I looked down at the ground below. I was with a nice, handsome man, and we had about an hour on a ride through nature on a beautiful, sunny day. Let the date begin!

We rode side by side for about fifty yards, until the trail took a turn toward the woodsy area surrounding the ranch. "Everyone will need to ride single file," the leader yelled from somewhere far ahead of us.

My gentleman-cowboy date urged me to go ahead of him. I urged him to. Ladies first, he insisted. I was desperate to make a good impression on this date—and a good first impression does *not* consist of a view of a woman's backside, spread the width of a big horse's saddle! Once I was ahead of him, I tried turning once or twice in the saddle to talk to Cal, but then my waist and neck started cramping, so I was forced to just stare ahead. What a view I had—two big butts: the rider's in front of me, and that of his horse.

My stomach clenched as I realized that was exactly the sight meeting Cal's eyes. And I had just begun to feel my back perspiring in the summer's increasing heat and humidity. I prayed the once-fresh T-shirt I was wearing did not have sweat streaks down the back. It felt like it was clinging to me. Did that mean my saggy back muscles were showing? Oh, this was not good.

A few minutes later, I realized it was better than what was to come. The stable hand had urged his horse into a trot. As I saw the helmets of the other riders ahead of me start moving up and down like a row of bobbleheads, I almost panicked. I heard Cal say something about how I better get my foot in the stirrup (aw, crap, he noticed that!), but Trigger was obviously a creature of habit and had broken into a trot along with all his other kin. So here I was trotting—make that *bouncing*—around on the horse like a sack of potatoes. I clung to the saddle horn and tried to balance myself with my left leg. My loose leg wasn't able to help balance me. The leg in the stirrup was straining hard to keep me upright, all the time actually slowly pulling the saddle—and me—to the left side. When I realized the saddle horn was no longer lined up behind poor Trigger's mane, I let out a shriek as I was bounced, inch by inch, closer to the ground.

I managed to pull the reins, and bless the horse, he stopped immediately. I kicked my foot out of the left stirrup, ignominiously got my right leg swung around, and managed to painfully slide off the saddle to the ground before the saddle slid portside anymore. I'll give Cal this: he had stopped his horse back far enough so I wouldn't have been run over if I fell off. He and the five or six others behind him were craning their necks to see what was going on. A few people hollered at me to see if I was okay. The rest, including Cal, were either laughing out loud or grinning. I was red-faced, and it wasn't from the heat.

Evidently there was another paid stable hand bringing up the rear. Almost immediately someone was next to me, adjusting both stirrups, tightening the cinch around poor Trigger's belly, and boosting me back up in the saddle before I had a chance to say that I'd be glad to walk the horse for a while. Like a conductor on a train, the helper yelled that we were all aboard now, and I was back to jostling.

Another humiliation was about to begin: Trigger's digestive system started to work right about then. I had no idea that the horse needed to go to the bathroom until

I suddenly heard a *phtt, phtt, phtt, phtt* emanating from his tail region in rhythmic time to the trotting pace we were on. Oh, man! I hoped no one thought those sounds were coming from *me*! Trigger and his musical tail continued the entire time we trotted.

At long last, my embarrassment was over. We emerged from the narrow trail into an open meadow, and everyone eventually gathered around in a circle. Trigger was able to relieve himself totally, and whether it was that, or just because we were all in a jumble, I noticed that Cal was on the other side of the group. I didn't care. I could see the stable way over on the other side of the grassy area, because we'd evidently ridden in a circle.

Trigger spied home, too, and seemed restless to get there. The group leader explained that if we wanted to break into a gentle canter the rest of the way, we should tap our horse's side gently. The horses knew there were oats waiting for them, he said. He also mentioned that if we wanted our mounts to walk, we should hold the reins tightly and the animal would plod on home.

I chose to plod. My neck and spine were stiffening up from the tortuous trotting they'd endured. Cal appeared beside me, and asked how I was doing.

"Great," I replied unenthusiastically. Sweat was running from the top of my helmeted head down my cheeks and disappearing into my now dusty T-shirt. I peered at Cal and felt a little better. He looked kind of like I felt.

"Good," he said. "I didn't know if you wanted to gallop back to the ranch?"

It was a question I think he was hoping I would answer with a no, and he got his wish.

I replied, "How about a walk so we can finally visit a bit?" He actually seemed relieved at that and swung his horse next to mine. At last!

One of the stable hands galloped up to us. "How are you doing, Tenderfoot?" he asked me.

"It's not my foot that's tender," I muttered. He just grinned, dug his heels into his horse's side, and shot toward the barn.

Evidently my docile Trigger took that as a challenge. Before I knew it, he'd sprung into a gallop as fast as the favorite out of the gate, taking me totally off guard. If I hadn't grabbed the saddle horn, I'd have rolled backward right off Trigger's rear. I guess my horse wanted to hurry home, get the saddle off, and receive his treat, because he took the bit in his mouth, and no amount of sawing the reins back and forth was going to slow him down.

There was something in Trigger's gait that made me wish that I had worn a sports bra. An extra-strong, industrial-strength sports bra, for that matter, would have been very welcome. I was swinging left and right, up and down, and flopping so much it was like there was a live mackerel on my chest. I was squeezing my legs so tightly against the horse to prevent me from falling off, that had Trigger been one of those thigh-toning devices, I would have crushed him.

At least we were getting to the end of this ride sooner rather than later. It was just embarrassing to see all the people who'd made it ahead of me watching me come in for a landing. But Trigger was on autopilot, and that included swerving suddenly to his stall and stopping dead in his tracks. My flopping top continued forward into the saddle horn, and I felt like I'd been punched in the gut. I sounded like I had, anyway: "Uuunnhhh!"

But I was done with the ride. I righted myself, and barely managed to swing off the saddle and slide to the ground. I almost sat down—my legs were like jelly—but I grabbed the horse's mane and made a pretense of petting and hugging him. I think I was actually hanging on to him for support for a few seconds. I finally turned to walk back to the main throng . . . and realized that there was no way I was going to be walking ladylike.

My cousin Jenny in Virginia had once colorfully described the first time she got off a horse, and now I knew what she meant. Yes, my legs were "as wide apart as a hooker's on opening night at a discount brothel!" I was mortified. The irony of it was that for years in my younger days, I had always done exercises designed to keep my thighs from touching each other. Now I'd gotten my wish, only about forty-eight inches farther apart than necessary. The only saving grace was that I was not the only one groaning in pain and walking spraddled.

I took off the sweaty helmet that had flattened my hair into a greasy-looking replica of itself, hitched up the stretched-out straps on my bra, and wiped my horse-hairy and dusty hand across my sweaty face. I decided right then and there I could never date a man whose choice of a first date sucked as badly as this date did. I didn't want lunch. I only wanted to get home and soak in the bathtub for hours.

Evidently Cal felt the same way. He was actually wheezing, and he apologetically and sheepishly suggested maybe we should call it a day. Riding in front of him most of the time must have made me miss his own equine ineptness, because he was soaked to the skin, and he had developed a goatee on his chin that hadn't been there before—courtesy, I assumed, from a face plant somewhere into his mount's dirty and shedding coat.

As we stood together, unhappily surveying each other, I thought he seemed a bit shorter than I'd noticed before. I realized that he was suffering the same thigh fate as I— only his legs were spread so much further apart, he had lost about five inches in height.

We each made it to our own cars, but not before we shook hands and confessed that maybe it had been more than a few years since we'd each ridden horses. Cal did try to regain some grace by mentioning he'd never ridden such a fat horse before. I just nodded, and mentioned that all the horses here seemed extraordinarily wide.

I had to sit in the car for a while before my legs stopped shaking so that I could drive home safely. I took a hot bath, some Minit Rub, Aleve, and suffered through a restless night's sleep before I was back to normal.

I never again heard from Cowboy Cal, but I checked his profile once. He had edited it. "Loves horses" was no longer there!

New Underwear-Worthy

My next date was for the Iowa State Fair. I'd never been to a live concert before, not counting any high-school band or orchestra concerts. My friend Big Bad John had once mentioned that he was a country-western fan when we had talked on the phone. I was not.

But when a relative gave me some free tickets to the Toby Keith concert, and they each included a backstage pass, I asked Big Bad John if he'd like to go with me. I heard heavy breathing on the other end of the phone, and it was not that he was excited to be going on another date with me. He was not only beyond thrilled that he would be getting to hear his favorite singer, but the thought of meeting his idol in person was evidently a real turn-on!

The big day arrived. BBJ actually drove all the way down to my place, pulling into my drive right before noon. I'm not known for my cooking—a fact that I had purposely left out of my profile—so I had agonized over what to fix for lunch, and decided lasagna would be something easy I could fix that would be edible. A premade salad, some garlic bread, and a beautifully set table were all ready.

After BBJ arrived, I proudly showed him that I'd made him lunch.

"Oh," he grunted.

I whipped my head up to look at him. Ouch! Darn, he was tall! "What? What's wrong? You haven't even tasted it yet." I was petrified that I'd made some horrible faux pas in food. "I usually just eat frozen diet entrees, but I thought *you'd* like this. Don't you like Italian?"

"Oh, that's not it," he said. "I'm sorry—I just assumed we'd skedaddle right over to the fair and eat up there."

"Oh!" It was my turn to utter one syllable. It was not the one-syllable word I *wanted* to utter. *Good grief!* I thought. *Here I slaved away to prepare an entire meal for someone, and all he wants to do is "skedaddle" and eat all that fried crap-on-a-stick stuff for which the state fair is famous.*

On second thought, that would have been fun, and really delicious. Darn, again. I shouldn't have assumed he'd want to eat anything I had fixed. My family had always made fun of my cooking. Maybe my bad reputation as a cook preceded me!

"Well," I said hastily, "I'll just put this in the fridge and I can freeze it later. Give me a minute and we can take off."

Evidently, my embarrassment was obvious, because BBJ showed some heart, and apologized. He insisted on sitting down and ate half a piece of the lasagna and several slices of the garlic bread. I kept eyeing the amount of food on his plate and his huge size and wondered how he could only eat a little bit. I was half his size but happily chowed down on twice as much as he ate, practically inhaling a large piece of lasagna. (I love anything with melted cheese in, on, or under it.)

But we ate fast in order to get to the fair, even though we had seven hours until the concert. I hustled out to the car and we took off. Forty minutes later, we pulled into a parking lot at the fairgrounds. A minute after that, BBJ got to witness his date having a meltdown. I had left the concert tickets at home!

Never have I been so thankful for the invention of the cell phone. After the sick feeling in my stomach subsided, I realized that we could drive all the way back to my place, retrieve the tickets, turn around, pay another ten bucks to get back into the parking lot and lose almost two hours of our date; *or* I could call my next-door neighbor, Joyce. She and her husband were not only going to the fair, too, but I had also gotten them tickets to Toby Keith's concert and they were going to meet us later. I just prayed that they hadn't already left.

Crisis averted! They hadn't left. Joyce let herself into my house, found the tickets where I told her I thought they would be, and then they were on their way. We were to meet at a beer garden in an hour.

BBJ and I wandered the fairgrounds. It's funny that in my hometown, I could go to a movie, a park, even walk around the neighborhood, and never see anyone I knew. But at an event like the state fair, with over seventy thousand people in attendance on one day, I saw people I hadn't seen in years!

Any person I saw whom I knew, I had to introduce to

my date. It was a given. My friends would holler hello to me, come running over like I was a long-lost relative, crane their necks to look up at my date's face, dart a look at me, then him, and then look at me with eyebrows raised. If they had just come right out and said, "Are you going to introduce me to this magnificent giant?" I might have beaten them to the punch. But I have to admit it was fun to watch their expressions. For people to whom I wasn't particularly close, I could tell they were processing the fact that the previously *single* Becky was with a *man*. Was he a date? A relative? Or was I just standing close to a total stranger?

I'd introduce him as my date who I'd met on the Internet, explain we were going to the concert, and watch as they raised their eyebrows again—both in joy for me, and approval that I had someone who (they thought) would spend that kind of money on me. I so wanted to say we had *free* tickets, but decided to let them keep their illusion. And BBJ just silently flashed his dimple at the women and let them admire him. I couldn't tell if he was embarrassed to be seen with me, just a bit introverted in public, or too busy checking out all the other people (read: women) who were walking around the fairgrounds in various stages of hot-weather clothing. He just kept pretty quiet and seemed to enjoy the view from up there.

We met up with my neighbors, my brother and my sister-in-law, and my nephew and his wife. All of them were big Toby Keith fans, and were also recipients of the free tickets and backstage passes. I gave both tickets to Big

Bad John for safekeeping, and soon it was time to go to the grandstand. We'd been instructed when to go to a certain gate for the VIP meeting with the star, Mr. Keith. I'd never been a "VIP" before. When it was announced for us to line up for our meeting, I noticed the jealous stares of people in the grandstand, and I'm afraid I kind of liked it! I began to pick up on all the excitement other VIPs had about meeting this famous singer. Evidently, he sang a song—or many—about beer drinking that was the favorite of everyone who was standing in line. BBJ even had several red cups he was going to ask him to autograph, and the people who saw them were a bit jealous. But when we got inside the waiting room, we were given instructions on what *not* to do or say to Toby. He was running late, and there was only time for small group pictures. We were forbidden to ask for autographs.

Fortunately for us, some of the other star-struck people in the waiting room were stars themselves: University of Iowa Hawkeye football stars. Both BBJ and I got our pictures taken with Chuck Long, former Hawkeye quarterback, and Ed Podolak, also a former Hawkeye, Kansas City Chiefs player, and radio commentator. Since I wasn't able to get Toby's autograph, Mr. Podolak graciously signed my red cup.

Then we were hustled in to meet Toby. I stood next to him while BBJ stood on my other side. I suddenly realized that probably during no other time in my life would I ever be able to call myself a MANWICH! Woo-hoo! We thanked Toby, he thanked us, and we left. But I was truly dazzled by his southern accent, his rugged handsomeness, and his star power. And the night was just beginning.

Before we got back to our seats, BBJ bought me a bottle of water, which I took a sip of and then put in my purse. The lid evidently wasn't on tight, a fact I discovered when I went to get my camera. My purse was soaked: cell phone, camera, and all.

BBJ just grinned at my embarrassment about yet another gaffe of mine. He had to bend down and yell in my ear because of the noise of the crowd, but he reminded me that the first time I emailed him my cell phone number, it was my daughter's, and that she had told him when he called "Well, she's blonde." Good grief. Why would he remember that?

I made it through the rest of the concert without a hitch, sometimes plugging my ears with my fingers, sometimes jumping up to clap along with everyone else, and sometimes just sitting still and wondering how much longer Toby Keith's vocal cords could last. It was almost midnight, and I had to work the next morning!

When the concert ended, my neighbors, relatives, Big Bad John, and I stood talking for a little bit. None of us seemed to want the evening to end. I felt like I had back in high school at prom—wide awake and ready to keep having fun. Both Joyce and my sister-in-law Erica had whispered to me that they really liked BBJ, and Erica even remarked that she hadn't seen me this happy in years. I was happy, but was it because of the excitement of meeting a star? I liked BBJ, but . . .

Finally, it came time to leave. My plans had been to ride home with my neighbors. Like a mother, I fretted that Big Bad John would have to drive so far when it was almost midnight. He'd been yawning for over an hour, and I was afraid he might fall asleep at the wheel. To be hospitable, I invited him to spend the night at my house—in my spare bedroom, of course. Even as I was saying that, my mind was racing. What on earth would I offer him for breakfast the next morning? I usually eat burned toast.

But (thank goodness, because I didn't know how clean my spare bedroom was and had never had a single male as a guest before), he declined. I had the feeling he might have been truly fond of me—the way a person was over an awkward, clumsy, into-trouble little puppy. He kissed me goodbye and explained he had to get home to pack up for his trip tomorrow.

"Oh, what trip? Where are you going?" I asked curiously.

He explained he was going to a neighboring state to see another woman. He'd had a date lined up with her for quite a while, and they had plans for the weekend.

Another woman? Out of state? For the whole weekend?

"Oh." It only took a fraction of a second, but I looked closely at Big Bad John then, and saw with my eyes what my heart had suspected all along about him: Here was a man who probably would always be looking at other women and making plans with them. My "mission objective" had changed somewhere along the dating line. I didn't want to date just to find a companion. I wanted someone who was looking for something permanent. What an epiphany!

That was when I decided for sure that I wanted to find a husband.

While I admitted that I thought of Big Bad John with affection, it was time to move on. I merely smiled at him, patted his arm, told him to have a nice trip, turned away from him, and never saw him again, although we did continue to correspond via email for a couple more months—as *friends*.

I rode home with my neighbors. As soon as I got inside my home, I nestled my wet phone in a box of rice (which really does absorb the wetness), opened up my Facebook page, and wrote about my night with a star:

*I am so excited about what happened earlier this evening! It was such a special occasion that I wish I'd gone out and bought all new underwear. I know you're thinking "new undies— **what?**" I grew up with a mother who, for every special occasion, bought us kids new underwear. I equate special occasions with new underwear. Any holiday, start-up of school, or even a family reunion, we kids got new underwear. I carry on that tradition. I'm weird that way, okay?*

Anyway, I had a date at the fair, and I think I'm in love. He's tall, blond, and can even sing. He definitely would have qualified as new underwear-worthy. He looked into my eyes and that was it—I was smitten. He's married, has kids, and is hardly ever home. But I don't care. I was positively lusting after him—yes, ME! Good Girl my whole life. Innocent, naïve Becky felt lust in her heart. I'm going to hell. I don't care. My eyes followed his every move. He moved with grace, masculinity, and the muscle liquidity of a panther on the prowl. (Prowling for me, I hoped!) He was beyond handsome. He was gorgeous. Beautiful. A Grecian God of a Thousand Ecstasies. What. A. Man!

Yes, along with thousands of other women, I'm in love . . . with Toby Keith. But unlike a majority of the people at the grandstand, I got to meet him backstage. In glorious person. And I'm a country-western fan now. Yee-Haw! I just hope I get my hearing back after the concert.

I left out the fact that I'd finally seen the light of day about Big Bad John. But I was content. With a new objective in mind, who knew what tomorrow might bring to me?

The End...Or, Rather, The Beginning!

Sometime before my Toby Keith concert date, I had walked my little dog Ralphie up the street to a retirement village. That neighborhood was peaceful, with beautiful flowers, brick duplex townhomes, and a lovely pond with a fountain. At the pond, a bench was set next to a weeping willow. It was a perfect place to just sit and ponder life.

Ponder, I did. I found myself thinking of life's big questions: *When would there be world peace? How long was I going to keep dyeing my hair, or should I let it go gray? What causes the stock market to fluctuate, and was it time I called my financial advisor? How on earth would I live without my kids close to me when they moved away next year? Do seniors get discount airline tickets? And what in the world was Ralphie rolling in right now?*

I also was thinking about all the new people I'd met during the past summer because of my online dating. Retrospectively, some of those thoughts made me cringe. Some brought a smile to my face, and some brought a smirk. Was this going to be what the rest of my life would be like? While I had met many interesting people, and made some new friends, online dating was also a lot of work. When I was sixteen, if a boy liked me enough to ask me out, it was an unwritten rule that all I did was tell my folks who I was going out with and where we would be. Because I wasn't dealing with a stranger, there was no need to do a background check, read anything at all about the boy, or worry about what kind of physical health my date was in.

I also found myself staring at the pond and enjoying the peaceful feeling of just sitting in the outdoors. That triggered memories of my lovely picnic date with Dave. Dave Andersen. For some reason, he was always in the back of my mind. *Why?* Maybe because he was a gentleman? Because he obviously was fond of me, even in love with me? Because he kept in touch with me through emails, always signing them, *Your friend, Dave,* so that I wouldn't be scared off like I had been after his passionate kiss? I wondered what would have happened if I hadn't had that tearful meltdown. At least I knew I had a life-long friend in Dave. We had lots in common, and not just that we had each lost a very beloved spouse. He made me laugh. We liked the same music, jokes, and types of people, and shared many of the same ethics. If I could only find someone like him, but with whom I would feel that romantic spark! Oh, well. *Que sera, sera,* as Doris Day would say!

When I left the pond and got back home, as if my thoughts of him had been magic, there was an email from Dave. Whoa! *Maybe I should start thinking of winning the lottery,* I thought. Dear Dave had sent another little email asking how I was doing, and was I going to be going to the state fair?

I sat down and answered him. Yes, I was, I told him. He knew I worked at Simpson College as a secretary, so I told him I was going to be working the college's booth in the Varied Industries Building on the Saturday following the concert.

Hey, I wrote. *I work there from eight until noon. If you want to go to the fair, would you like to meet me and we could walk around for a while?*

That would be totally "safe," at least as far as my feelings were concerned. I could drive up there, work, see my "friend" Dave for a bit, and then drive back home. He immediately wrote me back that he would love to see the fair, and if I wanted to catch a ride with someone, he would be glad to take me back home whenever I got tired of walking. Aww! Unbelievable that he was so considerate!

I wrote back that it would work out just fine, as long as he didn't mind driving all the way back to my home. I also mentioned that I had just been thinking of him and told him about the peaceful pond nearby. So I would have two dates for the fair: one for the concert with Big Bad John, and now one to actually explore the fair with my gentleman friend, Dave. This would be a good way to end the summer, I thought.

The Saturday following the Toby Keith concert, I rode up to the fair with a coworker, and we walked to our beautiful booth. Simpson is a small liberal arts college with about thirteen hundred students. I had worked there for twenty years. Our public relations/marketing department had, for the first time ever, put together a booth with all sorts of material about the school, free Frisbees, free water-based tattoos for the kids, and a "no-booth" photo booth that I was going to get to run.

The larger-than-life-sized screen was set in video mode so that fair-goers walking by could see themselves in live action. For those curious enough to stop, I would explain that the photo booth was a free and fun thing to try. I would position them in front of the screen, tell them to pose and count down from four to one, at which time the screen would freeze and snap their picture. Then they could pull icons available on the touch screen and "dress" themselves up with featured Simpson College colors, shirts, hats, and various other fun pictures. One older couple stopped to look, and as I visited with them, I learned they were from a nearby small town.

"I have a friend who lives there," I said. When they asked his name, I told them "Dave Andersen," and was surprised at the reaction I got from the lady.

"Oh, he is *such* a gem!" she exclaimed. She then proceeded to tell me all about his life as a single father after the death of his wife over a decade ago. To hear her tell it, Dave was a candidate for sainthood.

I debated a second, then decided to spring this news on her: "Well, I have a date with him later today."

Immediately, I found myself wrapped in a bear hug

amid cries of gladness. Then she pulled away and stared into my eyes with a little frown. She said, in a tone not unlike that of a math teacher announcing that there was an added question to a test that would determine failure or success, "He's Catholic, you know."

I nodded. "So am I."

She immediately gave me another joyous hug. You would have thought I was a heroine just returning from saving the world.

So when Mr. Andersen arrived a few minutes before I was to leave my booth duties, I was curious to see if he was going to look any different to me after that glowing review from his hometown friend. I saw him coming toward me, and his face split into a big smile when he saw me. We hugged, and then he asked me if I would like to walk around, or would I prefer to find some shade and sit for a while since I'd been on my feet all morning? (Was *Considerate* his middle name?)

I love television commercials, especially funny ones. At the time of my online dating, State Farm Insurance Company was running an ad promoting a pocket app. It featured a beautiful girl waiting for the date she met on the Internet—a "French model." As her date approached her, it was obvious to everyone but the young woman that he was anything but a French model. I thought this ad was hysterically funny and so clever.

So I copied it! When I was ready to leave my booth, I introduced Dave to all my friends. "I want you to meet my date. I met him on the Internet. He's a French model."

I wasn't sure if Dave would get the joke or not, but he passed the test with flying colors.

His eyes crinkled almost shut as he smiled, and then deadpanned, "BONE JURR!" My friends cracked up and seemed to be enthralled with him. Score one point for Dave.

We wandered around, talking, laughing, and eating some of the fair's delicacies that only appear once a year, and that I hadn't had a chance to have on Thursday with Big Bad John. I had to have a state fair corn dog. Corn dogs are sold in supermarkets in the frozen food section, and I tried some once. They were on par with the greenhouse-grown tomatoes you can buy in winter—there is no comparison to the real thing! Dave announced that corn dogs were his favorite treat at the fair. I looked at him with renewed interest.

I ran into my niece and her husband, and again introduced Dave as my "Internet French model" date. He knew his line, and we left my relatives, who were laughing with delight at the joke. We rode the Sky Glider and saw all the sights from the air. Then we wandered some more, finally sitting down beneath the shade of a tree.

We sat close together, and I felt as though I'd known him forever. I leaned over and kissed his cheek. He looked at me and grinned, then leaned over and gave me a quick kiss on the lips. I finally felt the spark.

The next day, Dave picked me up at my house and took

me to an ice-cream social. The night after that, he took me out to dinner, and kept doing that each night thereafter. Suddenly we were a couple, not just two people dating. I had no more interest in looking for a companion or friend. I had found something a lot better: I had found love again. My dating days were over.

Once again, I posted a Facebook entry:

What does a woman say to a man she's only had a few dates with who tells her he loves her and has since the moment he first laid eyes on her picture? Well, if you're a klutzy old blonde like me who recently watched a Toby Keith concert, you say "HAMMER DOWN!" I think that's cowboy talk for "Great"or "Wow!"

Yes, FB fans: I've chosen Cheesecake over sexy height. With my sweet tooth, was there ever any doubt? Big Bad John lost out to an oldster with the bluest, kindest eyes I've ever had the privilege of looking into. Maybe my subconscious had already picked him out, because he's the "Dave" that I kept calling Big Bad John on my first date with him! He's a widower with three grown children and two (and a half) grandbabies.

He reminds me of a leprechaun. (Have you noticed I can't ever just take anybody at face value for who they are—they always remind me of something else?) Besides the merry blue eyes, he has beautiful salt and pepper hair (a definite extra point in the follicularly challenged world of old men) and the cutest, most interesting face ever. He's soft-spoken, but when he speaks it's always about me—I have the sweetest smile, I have the prettiest hair, I have the best sense of humor, I'm a very special lady, yada yada yada! What's not to love about the guy? I wish I'd met him years ago—I could have made a fortune by tape-recording him and installing his compliments into hunky-looking robots that women could just turn on when they yearn to hear them!

Now that we're together, isn't there any sort of mature and distinguished word for a senior-citizen girlfriend? Would it be "lady friend" or "old dame?" Stay tuned!

My Facebook friends were both thrilled—and disappointed. They were so glad I had found someone, but as indicated by the vast number of replies on my Facebook account, they had been living vicariously through me! Once people had known I was on a dating site, they had asked me for hints or instructions for themselves or someone they thought might benefit from my experience.

Like me at the start of this adventure, they were looking for step-by-step instructions on how to date, or even how to find love. As with anything dealing with the heart, there isn't any one answer. All I know is, if an old klutz like me with hardly any dating experience can take a chance and find a match, I highly recommend online dating to anyone with the guts, desire, and dreams to handle it. It may help you find the love of your life. It may only give you some adventures you hadn't experienced before. Or it may not be for you at all. But just imagine feeling like you're sixteen again, and having the whole rest of your life before you. Sixteen: without the pimples, the curfews, or the inexperience. I think it's an adventure worth the effort!